The Uncovery is a Jesus-centered approach to dealing with addiction, mental health, and suicide that actually works because it leads us to the Father. George tells his story and the stories of those he has walked alongside with a raw, vulnerable edge that is eye-opening and deeply moving. Anyone who has ever struggled, hurt, or felt hopeless will be able to relate with his authenticity. This radical book lays out a solid framework for reflecting Jesus in culture while walking alongside those struggling or learning how to walk themselves without burning out or compromising truth in the process. Thank you, George and Brit, for "killing the noise" and saying what needs to be said in the recovery space. *The Uncovery* will not only change lives, I think it has the potential to help change the church as we know it.

—*Brian "Head" Welch*
Co-founder, Grammy Award-winning band Korn
New York Times best-selling author; costar, *Loud Krazy Love*

After reading through this book on recovery, I put it down, sighed in relief, and said out loud, "Finally, this book exists." It walks a tightrope between a fully faith-based approach to recovery with practical steps and perspective, and I really do think it's going to help many of you who read it or have family and friends who need language and tools who are recovering. I thought of different times over the years that I have had addicts live with me, and I attended rehab meetings with them to try and help them on their journey. I have always felt like there are big missing pieces in the narrative of recovery organizations, but I am so grateful that so many are working in this field. Along comes this book and the authors who wrote it together to inspire a new way of thinking that I believe will spark many models of recovery. It is a Christian message that gives hope for true healing and restoration, not just management of issues. I highly recommend this book and I pray that God uses it in a precious way.

—*Shawn Bolz*
Author, TV/podcast host, and minister, Bolz Ministries

The Uncovery is written by a man who's been through so much pain, addiction, and heartache. George shares his emotional story with a sense of humility and grace, never playing the victim but revealing victory through all the hell he's been through in his life. George Wood relates to the hurting and hopeless. No matter what you're going though in life, *The Uncovery* will bless you *immensely*!

—*Mario D'Ortenzio*
Founder, Death2Life.com

With a background of abandonment and a broken family, Pastor George Wood writes with wisdom and deep experience in what it means to be set free. *The Uncovery* will uncover your heart and expose you to His ways of love and healing. The principles George shares transform lives. How I wish the church world would embrace and adopt all that is contained in this book. It is a manual to living abundantly, a resource for leaders and counselors, and a gift to the body of Christ. Read it and be changed! And make sure you get a copy for a friend—they will thank you for it!

—*Brian Simmons*
Passion & Fire Ministries
Lead translator, *The Passion Translation*

The journey of recovery from things that keep us bound is at the very heart of the gospel. With refreshing honesty, George Wood and Brit Eaton invite all of us to understand and participate in discovering God's original design for our lives. *The Uncovery* is a powerful account of discipleship for those recovering from addiction, mental illness, or suicidal thoughts. Their teaching and George's firsthand experience of leading others into wholeness foster an ability to understand and implement discipleship in Jesus. *The Uncovery* respectfully challenges the church to embrace her calling as a community where all are invited into the transformative grace of Christ. The multitudes are coming, and we must prepare for those who are hungry to know the true and loving Father.

—*Bill Johnson*
Senior leader, Bethel Church, Redding, CA
Author, *Open Heavens* and *Born for Significance*

If you care about helping people recover from addiction, mental health issues, and suicidal thoughts, you simply have to read this book. George and team have figured out a model for recovery that works exponentially better than the status quo. Their extraordinary results demand your attention. I can't say enough about this proven, gospel-centric approach to recovery. Read, learn, and then go and do likewise!

—*Jordan Raynor*
Author, *Called to Create* and *Redeeming Your Time*

The Uncovery is such a timely and necessary book, not just for those who are in recovery circles, but for all who follow Christ. Wood and Eaton lay out a compelling and heartfelt invitation to do the hard, yet rewarding inner work—digging into our stories and opening ourselves to the tender, life-changing love of God. This invitation is not just for those who struggle with substance use. It is not just about getting sober. *The Uncovery* calls forth a new vision for the church to truly be a safe place for hurting people, which includes all of us. The lifetime journey of recovery is one of holistic transformation that requires community. Thank you for this sacred offering.

—*Bethany Dearborn Hiser*
Author, *From Burned Out to Beloved*
Director of soul care, Northwest Family Life

When it comes to recovery, it seems like we've seen the best that man can do. In this refreshing book, we are invited to see the best that Jesus can do by His scandalous grace. With honesty, insight, fresh language, and compassion, *The Uncovery* asks and answers some important questions for the church to see people made whole.

—*Jim Baker*
Senior pastor, Zion Christian Fellowship
Founder, WealthWithGod.com

At a time when disconnection and isolation seems to be a trend, George and Brit point out the importance of community, making this a vital resource not just for people struggling with addiction, but those called to lead and walk with them.

—*Bill Vanderbush*
Author, *Reckless Grace*

As I set this book down, one sentiment echoes in my mind: "Hurt people don't just hurt other people. They hurt themselves, too." It is an honest assessment of real life, and that is just what this book is—real. George Wood bore his chest, scars, and soul in this refreshingly authentic book, and nothing at all is sacred. His mistakes are our lessons, his sins are unabashedly on display, and yet his victories give us hope and stand to prove that we too can overcome.

—*Steven Christian*
Lead singer, Anberlin

The Uncovery is a must-have, go-to manual for everyone familiar with the broken road of addiction, hopelessness, and depression. In this riveting and compelling tell-all book, authors George Wood and Brit Eaton share their lives with complete vulnerability and transparency, unleashing fresh insight into healing and freedom. *The Uncovery* is a journey of pain becoming purpose, a story of a lost road becoming a roadmap for others still struggling on their journey. This book will stir you, move you, enlighten you, inspire you, and change you. You will be compelled to take it back to your community of fellowship/discipleship and watch it transform others.

—*John Skipworth*
Lead pastor, Oaks Church, Monroe, LA

This book removes the stigma of therapy (biblical Greek word *therapeuō*, *Strong's Concordance* G2323) by combining a practical approach to healing with a biblically strong foundation. *The Uncovery* represents the powerfully gentle way of how Jesus heals us all.

—*Norman T. Brown, Jr.*
Host, *Pneu Pneuma Godcast*

As a life coach working with young women struggling with abuse and mental illness, *The Uncovery* is a lifeline to my practice! Brit Eaton and George Wood boldly articulate the need for our understanding of addiction and mental illness, and then go on to show what the church and her leaders can do about it. We all know God's timing is perfect. *The Uncovery* has come at the perfect time. I am inspired by every word and recommend that anyone working with those who struggle with addiction, mental health problems, and suicidal thoughts grab their copy today! Let's work together to redefine what recovery looks like. I am so grateful that Brit and George answered the call to write this book. It is so needed!

—*Kristin Tucker*
Founder and director, Sacred Garden Foundation

Some ideas, maybe the best ones, are forged in the fire of experience. George and Brit have put into words what it takes decades of life, loss, and love to learn. *The Uncovery* is not just a way forward for those in search of sobriety; it is a real hope for all of us looking for community where we feel isolated and freedom where we feel bound.

—*Brian Sanders*
Founder, the Underground Network
Author, *Microchurches* and *The 6 Seasons of Calling*

George Wood is the boldest of the bold, tackling the most difficult problems of our inner cities—mental health, addiction, and suicide. He does so with an unbelievable level of commitment and selflessness. His story is personal and rooted in deep loss and grief but is an inspiration for many of us who have similar stories with family and friends. George and Brit now bring this message to the world so that recovery may truly be for everyone. Only one way he survives to write this book and that is with Jesus as his guide and rock. A must-read.

—*Jerry Dominic*
Executive pastor, Radius Church South Carolina

I love George's story. Our church used the Timothy Initiative to help build our coffee shop, so I've seen this ministry in action in real life. This book is not just another recovery book; it gets into the nitty-gritty of what George defines as the Uncovery. He does an amazing job of giving us tools to help others around us and get healthy ourselves because as he says multiple times, "Recovery is for everyone!"

—*Tommy "Urban D." Kyllonen*
Lead pastor, Crossover Church
Hip-hop artist and author, *Love Our City*

I heartily commend *The Uncovery* simply because it works in the real world where we all live. George Wood lives and loves in the real world. The Timothy Initiative and the Sober Truth Project both open the door to sobriety for broken men in the real world. *The Uncovery* is all about receiving the gift of fullness of life in the real world. Success in the real world, but how? Authentic family. Treasured communities. Following Jesus passionately. Uncomfortable vulnerability. Shocking honesty. Christ-focused. Holy Spirit-empowered. Abba-infused identity as beloved sons. Real revival, not the hype of running from one event to the next, but the deep embrace of life transformation. Jesus. Zoe life. Overflowing with grace and truth. Winning in the real world.

Eternal life means to know and experience You, Abba, as the only true God, and to know and experience Jesus Christ as the Son whom You have sent! Yay, God! Real life in the real world comes through real process. Enjoy your spiritual journey through *The Uncovery* and beyond.

—*Guy Glass*
Lead pastor, Cornerstone Mission Family, Tampa, FL

After knowing George Wood for the past few years, I can verify that every word in this book is lived out in his daily life. That's not the only reason I highly recommend this book. Being the leader of The Resting Place Church in Tampa, Florida, and seeing the men of the Timothy Initiative attend on a weekly basis, I can personally tell you that the process and approach described in this invaluable book *works*. I believe this offering is vitally necessary for the church of Jesus Christ today and the scientific community alike. The Spirit-breathed yet practical steps outlined within will challenge and equip you toward leading yourself and others into true recovery, the kind that the kingdom of God is looking for, the kind George and his community are truly living out. Read this expecting a deep conviction toward action, or don't read at all.

—*Caleb Hyers*
Pastor, The Resting Place, Tampa

Real recovery isn't about staying sober. Sobriety is just a side effect.

Jeremy Bogar | 3 years into the Uncovery

Before recovery, I was dead. The Uncovery transformed my life. Grace, love, and community keep me here.

Jonathan Hokes | 6 years into the Uncovery

Recovery is family. I couldn't have any length of sobriety, challenge, or a relationship with Jesus without my guys surrounding me.

Joe Carr | 6 years into the Uncovery

Recovery means real relationships. People who will always be there for me. That was so hard to come by before.

Saige Sheppard | 2.5 years into the Uncovery

Recovery is a new way of living. A new way of thinking. A new mindset with new perspectives on what's possible. Recovery is a whole new life.

Cody Cmero | 3 years into the Uncovery

For me, recovery is this beautiful opportunity to step outside of what my life was before. I had nothing then. Now I have everything.

Joe Surack | 3.5 years into the Uncovery

Real structure. Real accountability. Real community. *Finally.*

Michael Malpede | 6 years into the Uncovery

I found real recovery my first time—my only time. This new life is incredible and it's what makes me stick around.

Christian Lang | 6 years into the Uncovery

THE
UNCOVERY

THE
UNCOVERY

UNDERSTANDING THE POWER OF COMMUNITY TO HEAL TRAUMA

GEORGE A. WOOD & BRIT EATON

WHITAKER
HOUSE

THE UNCOVERY
Understanding the Power of Community to Heal Trauma

www.georgeawood.com
briteaton.com
www.timothyinitiative.org
sobertruthproject.org

The Timothy Initiative
3309 N 15th St
Tampa, FL 33605
(813) 537-5226

ISBN: 978-1-64123-853-3
eBook ISBN: 978-1-64123-854-0

Printed in the United States of America
© 2022 by George A. Wood and Brit Eaton

Whitaker House
1030 Hunt Valley Circle
New Kensington, PA 15068
www.whitakerhouse.com

Library of Congress Control Number: 2022936672

1 2 3 4 5 6 7 8 9 10 11 ᵾᵾ 29 28 27 26 25 24 23 22

DEDICATION

To my son, River. You're the reason I'm alive today. From the moment I looked into your eyes, I knew I would do anything to turn my life around and become the father you deserved. No amount of sacrifice, struggle, or hard work on my part will ever make up for the years we lost—and for that, I am sorry. My hope and prayer is that you see the man I am today—one who is committed to saving lives and restoring families so future generations won't have to struggle in the same ways we did.

Also to James, Sue, Kevin Jr., Alisa, Randy, Lionel, and Maria. I miss you every day. May your stories inspire others to choose life over death, in Jesus's name.

CONTENTS

FOREWORD

I sing in a band with my husband Josh. Before I wrote music with Josh, I sang in a band called Flyleaf for ten years. Some categorize our music as *hard rock*. But if I could invent a genre of music I like best, it would be the *honest* genre. There is something about honest music that is relieving.

Think of the honest genre like this: in this world of mask-wearers, someone just takes theirs off and emotionally vomits on stage. Something about that makes me want to cheer and laugh; it gives me a strange confidence to crowd surf. If this book *The Uncovery* were a song, I would put it in this category, in the honest genre. It gives me those same feelings.

My favorite thing about singing is looking out at a bunch of strangers and feeling this massive sense of unity and love toward them all. This book brings this sense too.

One of my favorite experiences in this life is feeling the love God has for people in my own chest. It is a mysterious gift from heaven. To look at someone, especially when they don't know how beautiful they really are, and see them through God's eyes is like being let in on a heavenly secret. But if you tell someone how loved they are, most times, they won't believe you. I know I wouldn't have before I met God.

People looked different the day after I met God. Wanting to die was all I could remember of my life before that, like a filter over every memory. When I was ten, my cousin was murdered. That's when I started hating everyone. I hated happy people for being happy in such a messed-up world. I hated healthy families for not being sick like mine seemed to be. I hated messed-up people for being messed up. My only hope, I thought, was death. Until I met God on the day I planned my suicide.

When I met God, every shadow in me fled from the light of His presence and I wanted to hide. But there isn't anywhere to hide from His light. I wanted to hide because He is Truth. Every lying thought that made up so much of who I was, was horrified to be a liar. He is so holy and I was so unholy. My whole being cried out, "You are the truth. I am a liar. You are life. I am dust and ash."

But a paradox came with this experience.

I understood: He is my Creator and I am His creation.

And so are you.

We are His work of art.

I was a blaspheming a work of His art. I had blasphemed every gift He had ever given in one way or another.

I sensed that I should not have survived that experience of meeting God. I woke up in my bed the next day, shocked that I was still alive. Later, I sat in my high school cafeteria and looked at all the people I had hated the day before and realized the truth about them. Each one was a gift to the world. Each one was God's artwork. The God of love and light and truth and holiness had created each person in the room by His love. I then began to be in awe of human beings. Every breath of each human, whether blasphemous or glorious, was a gift of mercy from the Creator.

It's one thing to love people who don't know this love of God, but it's another to love someone who does. That's how I realized

George Wood was family. I met him at a gathering of people talking about the mystical nature of God. We only spoke for a few minutes before I told him about my brother who was struggling with mental health issues and addiction. I don't remember how it came up, but I remember the way George lit up with love. Generally, people look at you with a sort of sad compassion when you talk about struggling family members. And in these circles, they may even give you some tips on evangelism or exorcism, both of which my brother had sought with little relief. But George was full of life and hope and a personal phone number to pass along to my brother. It was like immediately, my brother became his brother. Who does that? Someone who knows the love God has for people. It's knowing this love that makes us family.

When I read George's book that you are about to read, *The Uncovery*, I cried through so much of it. It describes what it is to literally walk through life discovering the depth and nuance of God's love for us and for others. Today, people think that passing off loved ones struggling with mental health and addiction issues to *professionals* is the only thing we can do. And the problem is such a massive epidemic that professionals and programs are overwhelmed with the numbers needing help. As George explains, deaths of despair—as deaths related to suicide, mental health, and addiction are called—are the number one cause of death in the world right now. In *The Uncovery*, George will teach you to walk alongside loved ones in their healing and recovery and be healed and recovered by the process yourself.

"We are all in recovery," George reminds us. This powerful truth humbles us to surrender our hearts to becoming a gift and enjoy the gift of others with whom we journey.

I recently walked through the pain of a loved one's suicide.

I had to forgive this person in my heart because of the pain they had caused me and so many people I loved by their choice. "I forgive you," I said out loud every time the pain came. There is a miracle in forgiveness. Memories that might have caused us to burn with anger can bring on tear-filled laughter instead. Like the time I had to help them through a drunken night of vomiting and prevent my children from hearing them argue with me about why they needed to keep their clothes on.

But I also questioned God, who had interrupted the first suicide attempt they had made and my two attempts to end my own life. He could have interrupted the last one of theirs. And yet He allowed their choice to be uninterrupted. I asked God about freedom. George points to my question many times in *The Uncovery*.

Didn't God use Moses to set the Israelites free from slavery in Egypt? But then many died while free in the wilderness. Didn't He want them in the promised land?

I know that without freedom, we can't truly love, but why is love worth the cost? Why give us freedom when we can use it to choose death?

I waited for His answer in silence until the memories flooded my mind. One after another after another, they came, these memories of my loved one who had taken their life. And every single memory was drenched in gratitude and love. As the slideshow went on in my head, God spoke to my heart: "People are worth loving no matter the choices they make."

Maybe you can read these words and be inspired by them. But when you live that reality out in your life alongside people, it will transform you into a promised-land citizen. It's one thing to love freely in ignorance, not realizing how painful it can be. I've done that and it leads to not wanting to love anyone anymore. It's another thing to love in obedience because you know it's right, but then you don't really give your heart because you don't want to get hurt. I've done that too, and it seems to be the smart response, but it has some gross and disappointing limits to it.

Many times, it can give a fragrance of disingenuousness to those we mean to love the most, and they may not receive our love in the end because they don't really feel loved and are not sure they can believe us. But there is another way to love. It is the way George writes about the Uncovery journey.

It is Christlike to love with full knowledge of the pain it could and will bring, to love with your whole heart and your whole yes. Loving someone is worth the pain. It is Christlike to believe and understand and experience the truth that people are worth loving no matter the choices they make.

When I read this book, I realized how important it is for this generation. So many are trying to make a big impact and stand up for the right cause, when really what we need so badly is for us to know how loved we are by God so we can love the one right in front of us. That's what George teaches you how to do with this book. That's what we need to know. That is the revival song we need to sing.

So read this book. Learn to be brave. Learn to be weak. Learn to be humbled. Learn to be confident. Learn to be loved. Learn to love. Learn to recover. Learn to uncover. Learn to be uncovered. Learn to live in the light and live *The Uncovery* journey.

—*Lacey Sturm*
Singer/songwriter and co-founder, Flyleaf

ACKNOWLEDGMENTS

To my mother and my sister Linda: thank you for moving past the pain into restored relationship.

To Will Barret and Matt Wallace, who took a chance to start the Timothy Initiative with me: thank you for helping me change lives.

To Jerry Dominic: your leadership and support carried me through so many years of struggle.

To Michael Maddux: your support since the beginning and your continued board leadership has been and will continue to be indispensable.

To my spiritual father, Guy Glass: thank you for showing me the love of a good Father God, the grace of Jesus, and the ways of the Holy Spirit to lead me into the kingdom of God.

To my T.I. community: Mike and Kristen, John (aka "Tree") and Casey, Joe and Lindsay, and Christian: thank you for believing big with me.

To my friends Kevin and Kathleen: thank you for journeying faithfully with me even when the road gets rough.

To Jason and Katy: without you two, there would be no Julie and me. Thank you doesn't even begin to cover it!

To Brian and Monica: thank you for giving the Timothy Initiative a home as part of your life's work.

To Pastor Doug: thank you for partnering and walking faithfully with me over the years.

To Pastor Tim: brother, our conversations of just how broken we both are have kept me humble.

To Bill Vanderbush: your message of reckless grace brought to life what was already inside of me. Thank you.

To Brad McCoy: thank you for reminding me that the still, small ways of Jesus have a big impact. It keeps me centered.

To my literary agent, Cheryl Ricker, and Whitaker House: thank you for taking a chance with me.

To Ricky George, Chris Bryant, Danny Marrs, Jeremy B, Joe S, Cole, Sage, Cody, and the hundreds of T.I. men who have walked alongside me: it has been my honor to journey with you.

To Armondo (aka "Pops"): thank you for leading me to Jesus and showing me the grace I needed when I was at the bottom.

To Julie, my amazing and beautiful wife: thank you for being my partner in bringing the kingdom. We have a lifetime of stories to live out together yet to come.

And to the person I could not have done this without, Brit Eaton. Thank you for taking my life's stories and turning them into something that will change and save lives! You're more than just my coauthor—you're my friend and partner in bringing this message of *The Uncovery* to the world.

INTRODUCTION

By the time I was in kindergarten, my father had abandoned me.

He'd already done all the fathering he wanted to do.

When I came as a surprise eight years after the last of my four older siblings, he responded with a fervent, "Thanks, but no thanks" and made plans to move on. He divorced my mother, left her penniless with three kids in upstate New York, and ran off to Florida with a much younger woman. My eldest brother Mark left with him, followed by my other brother James a year later, taking with them the last lingering thread of healthy male influence in my life.

Roughly a year later, Mark died in a construction accident in which my father was foreman, creating even deeper family resentment and division. My two sisters, Linda and Sue, left New York and joined my father and brothers to try and rebuild the family down south, leaving me and Mom in the dust.

These traumatic events changed how my parents viewed life—and how they viewed me—forever. To them, I was an inconvenience at best, a physical representation of a family that would never be. Even in his newfound freedom, Dad's hope faded quickly. His oldest son was dead, his girlfriend left him, and Dad fell into addiction. The summers I spent with him in Tampa were miserable. Mom did her best to pick up the pieces and make ends meet, but with nobody left to lean on but me—the reason my father left—she drank. A lot. My parents may have loved me in their own broken ways, but they no longer had time or space to parent me at all.

> MY BROKEN FAMILY SITUATION FUELED MY BROKEN IDENTITY. I FELT LOST AND ALONE, AND I WAS WILLING TO DO ANYTHING TO FEEL LOVED.

My broken family situation fueled my broken identity. I felt lost and alone, and I was willing to do anything to feel loved. It all came to a head one summer when my father's thirty-year-old girlfriend crawled into my bed late one night, drunk, and had sex with me. I was thirteen. From that defining moment forward, I thought sex *was* love, and alcohol was the best way to get there. So, like the confused kid I was, I went after it all. I began drinking and engaging in sexual activity with my peers. Women became objects, something to conquer and dispose of. Real relationships became foreign, which multiplied my pain and confusion. I balanced sports in middle school and high school with as much sex and alcohol as I could possibly get my hands on. Sports-related injuries led to three major surgeries, and those surgeries led to unmonitored painkillers. That careless mix of alcohol, sex, and opioids kept me so numb that I still can't remember most of the 1990s.

After the blur that was college, I graduated with my bachelor's degree and moved back to Tampa, where I partied with my father, my brother James, and my sister Sue on weekends. My sister Linda escaped the madness down south and moved back to New York, where she married and raised four unusually successful kids in an addiction-free home. But the rest of us delved deeper and deeper into denial about our struggles.

THINGS LOOKED GOOD ON THE SURFACE

I admit that on the surface, it looked like I had it all. I found a great job and built a successful career. I found a nice girl and married her, and we had a beautiful son, River. I was deeply addicted, but highly functional. Or so I thought. In 2002, I had a nervous breakdown—one so severe that I crawled inside a bottle of vodka for six months. My budding marriage, family, career, and life were dissolving right in front of me, and I felt powerless to do anything about it. My wife rightfully divorced me, taking my one-year-old son with her. I lost everything, including my will to live.

In the years that followed, my addiction, mental health problems, and suicidal thoughts owned me. I made genuine attempts at recovery, walking through twelve-step programs, rehabs, and counseling, many of them faith-based. I bulldozed my way through a trail of detox units and psychiatric wards, on suicide watch wherever I went. My ex-wife, newly remarried, did her best to honor supervised visitation with River, even though I was behind on child support. She showed me more grace than I deserved. But her confidence in me waned as I experienced relapse time and again. When a failed suicide attempt got me kicked out of rehab, she asked me to give up all parental rights and give our son a chance at a better life. I adamantly refused, but deep down, I knew she was right. He *would* be better off without an addict for a father. I would have been, too. I was coldly escorted out of yet another rehab facility without a clue about what to do or where to go. So, I tried something desperate—something I'd never tried before. Scuffling down the street with my entire life in a duffel bag, I cried out to heaven in desperation.

"God, either *kill me* or *do something*. I know this isn't funny to You."

Now, I always believed in God—but I also believed I was hellbound. It's what my parents told me. It's what the world told me.

It's what the church told me. I knew God existed, but I also knew He was *pissed at me* so I steered clear. Because I couldn't wrap my head around earthly relationships, I didn't yet understand that God loved me in a way no earthly father ever could. God met me in that last-ditch cry for help with a phone call. It was Luke, a Christian friend I'd met in a recovery house a few months earlier.

"Hey, man, are you okay?" he asked. "God told me to drop everything and call you right away because you needed help."

God had never been more real to me. And for the first time in my life, I wanted to know more about who He really was.

Luke took me in and introduced me to "Pops," one of his spiritual mentors. Pops introduced me to the *real* Jesus—the *real* way to the *real* Father.

A VICIOUS CYCLE

So, I got saved. And I got sober.

And I relapsed.

I got saved again and sober again.

And I relapsed again.

The vicious cycle continued as the words of all those well-meaning pastors, counselors, and recovery leaders over the years echoed in my mind.

Just come to Jesus, and you'll be okay.

Just come to Jesus, and you'll be set free.

Just come to Jesus, and you'll never use again.

Truth be told, I was about ready to have a come-to-Jesus moment with every single person who had thrown these quick-fix, phony platitudes at me.

Sure, I'd heard miraculous stories of altar calls and healing prayers that broke off addiction, mental health problems, and suicidal thoughts instantaneously and permanently. It was inspiring...but it wasn't my reality. Where was my miracle? Why was I relapsing? How could I get saved and sober, again and again, and still struggle? I started to doubt whether the kind of transformed life God was offering was really for someone like me.

Whenever relapse happened, Pops always saw it coming. He always gave me freedom to choose, and when I chose poorly, he was always there waiting to welcome me home and restore me gently. But in 2006, after a particularly rough go-round with the bottle, Pops laid it all on the line. Not with an ultimatum, but with a high-challenge, Spirit-led shaking.

"That's enough," he said. "It's time you realize God's grace has brought you this far."

That relapse was my last relapse. Pops became the loving earthly father I always needed, and God revealed Himself as the loving heavenly Father I never knew He was. And for the first time, I stepped into the transformed life He had waiting for me—a promised-land life worth staying sober for.

In 2007, I stepped into ministry as a recovery leader in Orlando and helped build a men's addiction program called Vision of God Ministries. When one of the other leaders relapsed, I was quickly promoted to the position of pastor and went all in with my call. I had a passion and a purpose for the first time ever. I helped broken men get free, I developed real-world construction skills, and I was able to provide at least some child support to my ex-wife for River. I stayed until the provision ran out—too long, in retrospect. I felt God leading me back to Tampa. But I had no plan. I had no money. I'd be crashing on Pops's couch. So, I had no choice but to lean completely on God to make a way for what He had called me to.

SUPERNATURAL ENCOUNTERS

Through a supernaturally timed series of encounters in a single weekend, God began to pull His plan together through His people. I met Carlos, one of my spiritual fathers, and his daughter Carla, who prophesied over me and invited me back into my true identity. I met Jason and his wife Katy, who became my best friends and ministry champions. I met George and Wendy, future benefactors, who hired me to provide live-in care and recovery services for their addicted son, David—in a million-dollar beach house on the Gulf of Mexico that was just five minutes away from where River lived. I couldn't have asked for or imagined a more perfect situation.

Once again, I was helping broken men get free. Once again, I was developing real-world skills and real kingdom connections. And once again, I was not only able to provide some child support for River, I was able to repay the full amount of child support that my ex-wife had deferred and forgiven me. Every single dime. She was overwhelmed by my transformation and moved with compassion to reunite me with my three-year-old son at the beach house. I'm forever grateful for her reckless grace to me. River, now attending Gustavus Adolphus College on a football scholarship, insists to this day that his first memories of me are in that peace-filled place. God did it all—and His grace was more than sufficient, even for me. So many people in addiction say they want to be a father. And when you trust God and let Him Father you, it creates a ripple effect that can change a family for good.

> WHEN YOU TRUST GOD AND LET HIM FATHER YOU, IT CREATES A RIPPLE EFFECT THAT CAN CHANGE A FAMILY FOR GOOD.

From that place of restoration and reconciliation, the momentum grew. I started helping the most desperate men I could find—many of them homeless heroin addicts who had been despised and rejected by traditional recovery programming. I was hired by an organization called the Underground to remodel an old furniture store into office space, and they encouraged me to hire the men I was loving and leading through recovery to help with the labor. I was able to offer them income, connections, and a renewed sense of purpose while working with and ministering to them daily, much like the apostle Paul and his protégé Timothy did. Even then, the Lord was equipping me to go deeper.

In late 2009, I began laying the groundwork for the Timothy Initiative, widely known as "T.I.," a community designed to house and empower men in recovery from addiction for as long as it takes to build a life worth staying sober for. The ministry launched publicly in 2010 and continues to thrive.

And then along came Julie—my wife, my partner, my equal in everything. I never dreamed I would be blessed with a second chance to be a God-honoring husband. But let me tell you, God is in the business of restoration. I'm convinced that the day He made me, He knew I would need her—and every time I see her, every time I watch the desires of our hearts come to life through the work of our hands, I think, *Okay, God, now You're just showing off.* When I married this smart, passionate, beautiful powerhouse for the kingdom in 2011, we became a family on mission. She too felt God calling her to a separate but parallel ministry path called the Just Initiative, which launched in 2015 as an organization committed to building community across typical economic and racial divides to create pathways out of systemic poverty for women and children at risk of homelessness.

Little did we know, God's collective call wouldn't stop there. In 2020, He birthed a third ministry, the Sober Truth Project. Our goal is to show the world the value of vulnerability over anonymity and total life transformation over baseline sobriety through education, advocacy, and practical support to help the world see recovery—and the role faith plays in recovery—differently.

Today, each of these ministries offers unapologetically Christ-centered, Holy Spirit-led transformation and hope for a promised-land life. Our goal is to change the way the world sees recovery so that people who are struggling with addiction, mental health problems, and suicidal thoughts aren't forced to do recovery in the margins.

> OUR GOAL IS TO CHANGE THE WAY THE WORLD SEES RECOVERY SO THAT PEOPLE WHO ARE STRUGGLING AREN'T FORCED TO DO RECOVERY IN THE MARGINS.

Recovery isn't just our ministry—it's our *life*. Julie and I actually live and work in the communities we've built together. We do every part of life with the people we've been called to love and lead through recovery. We own and steward multiple homes in underserved, crime-ridden, poverty-stricken, inner-city Tampa, where we all live together as family. We minister to the surrounding area, counseling, supporting, and advocating for hundreds more men and women who are actively building promised-land lives worth staying sober for. We're committed to living out an unconventional following of Jesus in a radical community lifestyle. And every precious life we see transformed by God's grace provides consistent affirmation that Julie and I are exactly where we're meant to be.

We know this all-in way of life is not for everyone. You may not be called to a radical sober-living community on mission like we are—and that's okay. But if you're called to love and lead people through recovery in an age of unprecedented isolation and desperation, you will be called to go deeper, to see recovery differently than you ever have before. Deep down, you probably already know that, or you wouldn't be holding this book.

It's time for us to take a comprehensive look into what's working (and what's not working) in recovery and humbly ask God what more He would have us do. I'm confident that the insight He continues to reveal in and through our ministries will transform modern recovery as we know it. It's my honor to share some of those insights with you in the pages of this book.

So, let's do this. Let's break out of the recovery mold, tap into the abundant life Jesus died for, and reveal the truth about who God is—and who we are in Him—once and for all. Welcome to *The Uncovery.*

PART I

REDISCOVERING RECOVERY

Christian recovery has come a long way. Since Alcoholics Anonymous created the first broadly known, widely embraced "safe place" to focus on sobriety in the 1930s, both secular and sacred organizations alike have improved by leaps and bounds to protect the dignity, health, and lives of people who struggle not only with addiction, but also with mental health problems and suicidal thoughts. And yet the struggle remains so real for so many—more than you might realize.

Unfortunately, recovery as a process is limited. The very nature of the root word "recover" means to get back something that has been lost. But even the best programming can only recover *a broken life* that drove us toward our struggles in the first place. Why would anyone want *that* life back? There has to be more.

Recovery becomes increasingly complex in a post-pandemic world, where the old life we once had is no longer available. Addiction, mental health problems, and suicidal thoughts are consuming society like never before in the aftermath of extended global quarantines. More people are struggling and sharing those struggles openly, but the world is ill-equipped to embrace them. This is why we so desperately need reform in recovery—to welcome and introduce the struggling to Jesus, who is Hope Incarnate.

Wild opportunities for hope, healing, and transformation exist in the Christian recovery space because we're not recovering an old, broken life—we're going after a brand new one. *"The old has gone, the new is here!"* (2 Corinthians 5:17). As we choose to do recovery differently, the sons and daughters of God discover the truth about who they really are. Finding freedom. Experiencing transformation. Building an abundant life. It's what we call *the Uncovery*.

1

REDEFINING RECOVERY

Dear friends, let us love one another,
for love comes from God. Everyone who loves has been
born of God and knows God.
—1 John 4:7

Two months. That's all the time it took for the Israelites to relapse. Fresh off a miraculous delivery after four hundred years of generational slavery under Egypt's hard-hearted pharaohs, God's chosen people stepped into freedom for the very first time.

The first leg of the exodus journey was filled with songs of endless thanksgiving and praise. Their voices rang out, *"I will sing to the LORD, for he is highly exalted"* (Exodus 15:1). But the realities of hunger and uncertainty hit them hard...and the people started to grumble. They told their leaders, Moses and Aaron:

> *If only we had died by the LORD's hand in Egypt! There we*
> *sat around pots of meat and ate all the food we wanted, but*
> *you have brought us out into this desert to starve this entire*
> *assembly to death.* (Exodus 16:3)

We can only imagine the other icy remarks whispered under their breath:

"Delivered from slavery only to starve to death. Thanks a lot, Moses."

"If God promised us this land, why should we have to fight for it?"

"I'm so sick of manna. Can't we get some lentil stew?"

"Maybe being a slave wasn't so bad after all."

"Maybe we should go back."

This newfound freedom was *not* going well for God's chosen people. Though physically free from bondage and oppression, they were still slaves at heart. And when you try to tell a lifelong slave that they're not only free but family, it's going to take a whole lot more than platitudes, prayers, and twelve-step programming for them to believe it's true, let alone embrace the new life that comes with it.

If you've read or skimmed through the early chapters of Exodus, you'd probably agree the Israelites were suffering from some serious short-term memory loss. Umm, no—they likely didn't eat their fill of meat in Egypt. They were slaves whose lives were *"bitter with harsh labor"* (Exodus 1:14), and when their numbers grew, Pharaoh ordered the midwives to kill baby boys, which they secretly refused to do. (See verses 16–17.) Who in Pharaoh's regime would have given two thoughts about whether they'd eaten their fill of meat?

SATAN LOVES TO TRICK PEOPLE INTO THINKING THEY SOMEHOW HAD IT BETTER BEFORE THEY WERE SET FREE.

Satan loves to trick people into thinking they somehow had it better before they were set free. When he does, they forget the brutality and romanticize the past. *We got three square meals a day in Egypt! We're missing out!* Come on. This demonic fear of missing out not only causes people to grumble and stumble, it causes them to relapse into old, broken ways of thinking and behaving.

In their wild, decades-long pilgrimage, the Israelites experienced deliverance, miracles, and provision that should have given them hope for the future in a promised land they could inhabit and call home. But time and again, when the going got tough, the tough didn't get going. They threw a pity party. They slandered, schemed, and spewed hate against Moses, Aaron, and the God who set them free. Faced with all-new challenges, they looked back longingly at the days when things certainly weren't better but at least they were a known quantity. And when they learned there might be *giants* in the promised land they were about to inhabit? Many stubbornly dug in their heels just shy of the hope-filled future right in front of them. Dragging their feet, clinging to what they knew, the Israelites ended up wandering in the wilderness for forty years.

Moses had been called to not only to deliver his people from Egypt but also to empower their transformation. This required sacrifice. It required relinquishing his pride and ultimately his life. From the burning bush to the battlefront, the exodus encounter was never about what Moses wanted. It was about what God had planned since before the foundation of the earth and what He orchestrated in His perfect timing. Despite the opposition of Moses, Pharaoh, and His own chosen people, God still got what He wanted—for our good and His glory.

DELIVERANCE IS NOT DESTINATION

When freedom from bondage comes miraculously and instantaneously, as it did for the Israelites, it's important to remember that deliverance isn't the ultimate destination. It's the start of a journey toward hope, healing, and total life transformation. When people can't see the potential for that new life, they will go back to what they know.

> WHEN PEOPLE CAN'T SEE THE POTENTIAL FOR A NEW, PROMISED-LAND LIFE, THEY WILL GO BACK TO WHAT THEY KNOW.

This is especially true in recovery. Relapse is not only possible but probable for most people who struggle with addiction, mental health problems, and suicidal thoughts, which leaves little room for perfectionistic legalism in our recovery programming. Whether Christian or secular, inpatient program or twelve-step meeting, sobriety (deliverance) is all too often glorified over transformation (a promised-land life), producing a multitude of dry drunks and generational slaves who don't yet know they're free. Lives and souls are at stake—more than we know. It's time for God's people to go deeper.

Here's the sober truth: *Getting sober is only the beginning.*

Getting to the promised-land life God has for all of us requires potential for a life worth living—and worth fighting for. People recovering from addiction, mental health problems, and suicidal thoughts don't always have the means or the ability to build such a life on their own. Perhaps they can't even imagine such a life is possible. We were never meant to do recovery on our own.

This is true of my own life's journey. As the product of a broken and divided home and the youngest of five siblings, the world might have expected an overlooked, undervalued kid like me to struggle with drugs, alcohol, and mental health problems. My parents and siblings did, so why not me? Thankfully, God had other plans—not just for my sobriety, but for a promised-land life on the far side of the wilderness.

And yet I decided to put those plans on hold, again and again, to go back to what I knew, back to who I thought I was. Just like the Israelites, I've done my time in the wilderness. I've stared longingly across the Jordan into the promised land without the strength or courage to take the first step. I've been to hell and back again since my initial deliverance, but God never lost His hold on me. After a decades-long cycle of addiction, I felt the Father calling me into something that seemed simple on the surface. He called me to help men like me get free. It may have been simple, but it certainly wasn't easy.

Building three radically different—and occasionally divergent—recovery ministries goes hand in hand with personal sacrifice. It was true for Moses, and it's still true for Julie and me today. Going beyond programmatic sponsorship relationships into true discipling relationships ended up costing me and my family more than I ever could have imagined. If I'd known just how much, I might have said no.

On July 3, 2009, when the Timothy Initiative was still an ill-formed idea in my mind, my sister Sue died of a drug overdose. In a desperate season of life, she tested positive for HIV and hepatitis C, and her Interferon treatments escalated her preexisting mental health problems. Sue's death lit a fire under me. The surface-level lay ministry I'd been doing for the kingdom was only scratching the surface of what God was empowering me to do. So I dealt with the pain of Sue's death by doing something about it. I fleshed out a strategy, filed for nonprofit status, quit my day job with the Underground, mobilized volunteers, and went all in to build the Timothy Initiative.

Things were fast and furious in my own strength over the next six months as we brought T.I. to life. But on January 17,

2010—just days before the ministry's official public launch—my brother James also died of a drug overdose.

James certainly didn't fit the "addict" mold. He excelled academically and professionally. With a 4.0 GPA in college, law school at Stetson University, a Master of Laws from the University of Boston, and a fierce work ethic, James landed a prominent position as an attorney in Tampa, where he was about to make partner. Despite his outward successes, however, his life had become more than unmanageable. A high achiever who couldn't maintain the success he'd grown accustomed to, addiction and depression consumed him. After being prescribed unmonitored Oxytocin for routine knee surgery, James leveraged his legal authority with local doctors to score more and more medication in the *pill mill* that was Tampa in the early 2000s. Only a handful of people, myself included, knew James had previously threatened suicide. And although he left no note, he slipped away surrounded by photos of family and loved ones spread across his bed.

How could this happen? My identity was shaken to the core. I had been so sure God set me free so I could set others free—and I couldn't even deliver my own family from bondage. I wrestled with my reality, wondering if I had misunderstood God's call to recovery ministry—or worse, if God had somehow made a mistake by choosing me. As I confessed this to a pastor friend, he shared a Scripture verse that would become a cornerstone for my life.

> *They triumphed over him* [the accuser] *by the blood of the Lamb and by the word of their testimony; they did not love their lives so much as to shrink from death.*
>
> (Revelation 12:11)

I took that prophetic word to heart, and the formational years of T.I. were incredible. God's hand was everywhere—in miracles, provision, transformation, and powerful moves of the Holy Spirit. We saw men like me set free. They not only got sober; they stayed that way. The collective transformation was undoubtedly miraculous; I knew we had tapped into something supernatural.

But like many first-time leaders lacking in wisdom, I started to get out of step with God. I compensated for my lack of competence by pushing harder to be the change I wanted to see in the recovery space. I became angry, disillusioned, and hypercritical of faith-based recovery, convinced I could figure out a better way on my own. Exhausted, my confidence waned, and my boundaries crumbled. Five years into the Timothy Initiative, I hit a wall. Relapse was imminent, and the underlying emotional and physiological issues that enabled my addictions in the first place were bubbling up to the surface under stress. I was terrified to let anyone see that I was struggling, failing even, blindly leading the blind toward the edge of a cliff. If they found out, I'd lose everything again. My marriage, my ministry, maybe even my life.

During this refining time, God told me straight-up that my sobriety alone wasn't going to cut it anymore. He wanted my whole heart, every part of my life. He wanted to bring me all the way home to a promised-land life—one that was not only worth staying sober for but worth fighting to defend. Only from that place of healing and wholeness could He use me to invite others to go deeper into their own recovery—to seek not only sobriety, but also to believe for and work toward total life transformation. I didn't have to be perfect. But I had to be surrendered.

So, I did the hard work. I confessed my struggles to my leaders, and they were thrilled to see me leaning in instead of looking for a way out. I started seeing a therapist and attended a twelve-step program for sex addicts, earning a one-year medal. But I didn't stop there. I also pursued deep inner healing at a globally recognized seminar, where I experienced a supernatural shift that transformed my heart and life forever. Once that healing happened, I had to be ready to move on to what God had next for me. After all, how many times can you retrace twelve steps and still uncover the next level of healing? This revelation changed everything for me—and it's helping people like me get and stay free.

It's been millennia since the exodus encounter, and the captives and prisoners we Christians deliver from bondage in Jesus's name are still teetering on the edge of promised-land life transformation far longer than they need to. Recovery program fail-out rates are downright sobering.

Case in point, research shows as many as 40 percent of people drop out of the Alcoholics Anonymous twelve-step program in the first year.[1] Some addiction specialists believe program success rates are between 8 and 12 percent.[2] AA's self-published *Big Book*, however, boasts a 50 percent success rate.[3]

PARTICIPANTS MAY NOT ALWAYS ADMIT IT WHEN RELAPSE HAPPENS, MAKING IT NEARLY IMPOSSIBLE TO QUANTIFIABLY PROVE THE EFFECTIVENESS OF ANONYMOUS PROGRAMS LIKE AA.

The reality is, participants may not always admit it—let alone report it—when relapse happens, making it nearly impossible to quantifiably prove the effectiveness or ineffectiveness of such anonymous programs. Add Jesus as "higher power" into the mix, and the numbers, sadly, don't get much clearer. Powerful testimonies and wildfire success stories take center stage and go viral, while the majority still suffer in silence. In divergent recovery ministries like

1. Scott O. Lilienfeld and Hal Arkowitz, "Does Alcoholics Anonymous Work? For some heavy drinkers, the answer is a tentative yes," *Scientific American*, March 1, 2011, www.scientificamerican.com/article/does-alcoholics-anonymous-work.
2. Jeannine Stein, "Charlie Sheen claims AA has a 5% success rate—is he right?", *Los Angeles Times*, March 3, 2011, www.latimes.com/archives/la-xpm-2011-mar-03-la-heb-sheen-aa-20110302-story.html.
3. American Addiction Centers Editorial Staff, "AA Success Rates," December 30, 2021, rehabs.com/blog/aa-success-rates.

the Timothy Initiative and the Sober Truth Project, our so-called *failure rates* are almost nonexistent. To be fair, it's because we're not going after baseline sobriety—we're believing for total life transformation. Sometimes it takes twelve steps. Sometimes it takes a forty-year journey. We need to be ready and willing to walk alongside people in recovery for as long as it takes.

Now, please don't hear what I'm *not* saying. I love Alcoholics Anonymous, Narcotics Anonymous, and Celebrate Recovery. I love clinicians, counselors, and mental health professionals. I love any group of people making a concerted effort to help break the chains of addiction, whether or not a faith component is involved. I regularly partner with and work alongside these groups to share resources and offer more comprehensive care for the people I'm called to love and lead. That being said, when the end game in recovery programming is to "stay sober," the data shows people will inevitably go back to what they know.

Our western American culture is more comfortable with vulnerability than ever before. But the sting of stigmatization still surrounds people in recovery, even in the one place they deserve to feel safe: the church.

Ben, one of my closest friends and confidantes, is one of the few people in the world I can run to when I struggle. It's not because he's a solid Christian who always has the right Bible verse to throw at me in times of struggle and temptation. In fact, Ben is an agnostic. I go to him because he's been loving and leading people in recovery for even longer than I have—and he intimately understands the unique challenges that long-time-sober recovery leaders face. He knows what it's like to be sober for more than twenty years and still struggle because he's living it with me. To be honest, Ben has proven that he offers a safer space than most of my Christian recovery contemporaries. It's sad but true. Ben sees and loves me for who I really am—and he's willing to receive me without judgment, just as I really am. I never have to get myself together before I go to see him. He doesn't believe in what he calls my "big-G God." But Ben loves unconditionally like our Father does and initiates with grace like Jesus. Sometimes I wish my church friends could be a little more like Ben.

Like the Christian church, I believe recovery is in desperate need of reform. And I believe it's the church's responsibility to bring that reform from the inside out. This reformation, like any other, will take sacrifice. It will require us to let go of our preconceived notions about recovery and the people in it. It will require stepping beyond our go-to, faith-based and secular programming models, bridging the gap between Spirit and science. And you'd better believe it's going to require an untangling of our broken theological ideologies to discover a God who is even better than we think He is.

UNPACKING THE UNCOVERY

It's time to take a hard look at what's working—and what's not working—in modern recovery. Throughout the pages of this book, you'll see me use the terms "recovery" *and* "the Uncovery" almost interchangeably and for good reason. Recovery is part of the Uncovery, but the latter does not fit within the traditional recovery mold. Our goal isn't to replace the word "recovery," but to expand upon the concept and look at it differently.

RECOVERY IS THE WHAT

Recovery is what we're doing and what we want—to get free of addiction, mental health problems, and suicidal thoughts for good. A catch-all term, recovery is a word widely used to describe both a process *and* a desired outcome, leaving people who are "in recovery" in a perpetual state of uncertainty, wondering, *Am I recovered yet? Is being recovered even possible? And if not, why am I still trying?* For some, a twelve-step program, a detoxification program, and even sheer willpower can propel a person into recovery territory. But for the majority of struggling people, experiencing life transformation takes more. If we're going to love and lead people *through* recovery, we must first believe that crossing over to the other side is possible.

THE UNCOVERY IS THE HOW

More Spirit-led exploration than hardcore process, the Uncovery is a deep-dive excavation into what grace-filled, Christ-centered recovery was always meant to be. The Uncovery is not lockstep, programmatic, or sequential—it looks different for everyone. It goes beyond maintaining sobriety to building a transformed, promise-land life that's worth living. The Uncovery encompasses recovery, but it also invites us to go deeper and do more in the recovery space, both for people in recovery and the ones loving and leading them through it.

Still with me? *God love you.* We're heading into uncharted territory together. It won't be easy. But I know it will be worth it—for me, for you, and for every single person for whom Jesus died.

WHAT RECOVERY ISN'T

Recovery is one of the most widely misunderstood concepts in modern culture. Even as you dig into these pages with a deep desire to learn, you likely carry a preconceived notion about what you think recovery is—or isn't. In my experience, the learning process often requires us to *unlearn* what we thought we once knew so we can *relearn* it in its proper context. It can be emotionally charged work, especially when we cling to our ideologies too tightly. But deep down, we know it's humility that positions our hearts and minds for growth. So let's get the unlearning process started—not with what recovery *is*, but what it *isn't*.

When Jesus walked the earth, healing was high on His priority list. Blind eyes were opened, deaf ears were unstopped, lame people leapt, and the speechless shouted for joy, just like the prophet said they would. (See Isaiah 35:5–6.) More so than itinerate ministry or table flipping, Jesus loved to heal—and He did it just about everywhere He went. But when Jesus healed, He didn't always do it in the same way.

Let's focus in on one of His favorite types of healing—blind eyes. A single touch from Jesus was all it took to heal two blind men. (See Matthew 9:27–31.) This kind of instantaneous healing inspires grateful remembrance and worship song lyrics.

Beautiful, simple, elegant, and above all, church-appropriate. When can we schedule the next healing, Jesus?

Sometimes healing blind eyes required a muddy mix of dirt and Son-of-Man saliva to make a healing mask, as it did for a man born blind in John 9:1–7. This kind of healing is probably a little messier than most of us would like, including that blind man.

We appreciate the healing, Jesus—but who's going to clean that up?

Sometimes it took Jesus spitting straight into your eyes and laying hands on you—more than once!—like it did for the blind man at Bethsaida in Mark 8:22–26. Spitting and second chances can come off a little reckless for some churchgoing folk.

Okay, Jesus—thaaaaaat might have been a little too much. We are in church, you know.

Jesus's wild variety of healing styles demonstrate that God's grace doesn't always look like we think it should and that progressive deliverance is not only a possibility, but a promise. Apply this truth to recovery, and you'll realize it's high past time to diversify our approach.

RECOVERY ISN'T A ONE-TIME EVENT

If you've been in recovery circles for any length of time, you've probably heard inspiring testimonies from people who were delivered from bondage *straight* into a promised-land life. They may have said something like, "I met Jesus and I never touched the stuff again!" One touch was all it took. And they all lived happily ever after. The end. We sit on the edge of our seats and soak up these testimonies but wonder why they're the exception instead of the rule in our own experiences.

Now, I certainly believe God *can* and *does* heal addiction and mental health problems instantaneously and miraculously. Scripture proves it. I've seen and personally experienced it. You'd better believe I'm *believing for it*. But I also believe God values the recovery journey as much if not more than the moment of deliverance. It's like falling in love—it looks different for every person and every relationship, in every stage. It's always miraculous, but never formulaic. It takes us by surprise and makes us want to go deeper. It always reveals our God-given identity.

> THE UNCOVERY BORES DOWN DEEP BENEATH THE SURFACE, ALLOWING ANY UNDERLYING ISSUES TO BE NAMED AND DEALT WITH PROGRESSIVELY IN GOD'S PERFECT TIMING.

The Uncovery bores down deep beneath the surface, allowing any underlying issues to be named and dealt with progressively in God's perfect timing. (See Mark 8:22–26, Luke 17:14, 2 Corinthians 3:18.)

RECOVERY ISN'T A PROGRAM

Twelve-step meetings, inpatient rehabilitation centers, and self-help practices all have their places in recovery. I'm not against giving time-tested, time-bound solutions a shot, especially in the early days of one's sobriety. But the problem is, one-size-fits-all, mass-produced, secret-sauce programming gives far too many people whiplash, bouncing between sobriety and relapse. This vicious cycle leaves people on the outside looking in, until the unbelonging they feel becomes too painful to bear and they give up.

I'm living proof that the recovery system doesn't always work the way we think it should. Some of us need a level of Holy-Spirit intervention and Christ-centered community that even the best systems and programming just can't offer. There's nothing wrong with organization. God is a God of order. But real recovery transcends organized, manmade processes for organic, supernatural growth.

> THE UNCOVERY NEVER ASSUMES WHAT WORKS FOR ONE PERSON WILL WORK FOR EVERYONE. EACH RECOVERY JOURNEY IS AS UNIQUE AS THE PERSON BRAVING IT.

The Uncovery never assumes what works for one person will work for everyone. Each recovery journey is as unique as the person braving it. (See Matthew 10:29–31, Jeremiah 29:11, Psalm 119:73–74.)

RECOVERY IS NOT ASSIMILATION

This is an especially difficult concept for the church to grasp because it's how the church has incorrectly (and perhaps inadvertently) structured and mass-produced discipleship programs over the years. Whether we're disciples who make disciples or healed people who heal people, we can be easily tempted to believe the lie that we all must look, think, act, and behave in exactly the same way. This only further alienates those who cannot or will not assimilate. Unity does not—and should not—mean uniformity.

All too often, we stress behavior modification to push our own broken agendas. We strip away labels like "addict" and "suicidal" only to slap on new labels that sound more like the ones we've placed on ourselves. We might even suggest anonymity become a thing of the past—not to invite people to walk in the light as Jesus is in the light, but so we can expose secret and not-so-secret sinners in our midst, thereby encouraging believers to keep their struggles between themselves and God. This is not Christian recovery—it's toxic Christianity.

> **THE UNCOVERY IS A UNIFYING JOURNEY THAT CELEBRATES DIVERSITY AND COMBATS STIGMATIZATION AND DISCRIMINATION, MODELING THE GENTLE WAY OF JESUS.**

The Uncovery is a unifying journey that celebrates diversity and combats stigmatization and discrimination, modeling the gentle way of Jesus. (See Galatians 3:28, James 2:2–4, Mark 12:31.)

WHAT RECOVERY IS

Now that we've unlearned what recovery isn't, let's relearn what it is:

+ Recovery is life.
+ Recovery is the gospel.

More than a replicable lifestyle or series of behavior modification techniques, real recovery is the discovery of a person's God-given identity and learning what it means to walk in it for the rest of your life. This is hard if not impossible to do anonymously. It requires a Spirit-led, relationship-driven approach that in many ways cannot be programmed. Operating not in a rigid process but a flexible framework can provide opportunities for people to go deeper in recovery—into Uncovery territory.

THE UNCOVERY

In my work with the Timothy Initiative, our approach to helping broken men transform is founded upon a person's whole life, including spiritual discipleship, recovery, community, work therapy, and more. By exploring and diving deep into each of these areas of life, we can provide a unique prescription for healing and wholeness that creates pathways to a promised-land life. The Uncovery's multifaceted, relational approach looks at the fullness of the individual, not just the struggles from which they're attempting to recover.

SPIRITUAL DISCIPLESHIP

Sure, you can get sober without Jesus. But building a promised-land life worth staying sober for is not possible without a firm foundation in Christ. People in recovery need to hear the truth of the gospel in language they can understand, grow from, and eventually share with others. Discipleship is all about helping people get to know the real Jesus—not just knowing about Him but knowing Him personally.

SOBER LIVING

Recovery is just one part of the Uncovery. Getting to the root of addictions, mental health problems, and suicidal thoughts requires a deliberately comprehensive approach. This means honoring the whole person by removing labels and helping them walk through deeper-layer struggles as they come up along the journey—and believe me, they will. It's about learning new patterns of living to move beyond sobriety toward a transformed life.

COMMUNITY

Authentic community is the all-too-often missing piece in the recovery puzzle. While Friday night meetings and weekend service projects present opportunities to build real friendships, they can also be a breeding ground for triggers and codependency. We need to relearn what it means to do life together in an atmosphere of transparency, vulnerability, and unconditional love that leaves no one behind.

WORK THERAPY

People in recovery need a purpose, and work can be an important reason to stay sober. Helping people find and keep jobs they enjoy doing builds dignity, responsibility, knowledge, and experience. And if we can't help them find jobs, why not create them? Startups and microbusinesses can provide income opportunities and entrepreneurial training for people in recovery who want and need to work in a safe, supportive environment.

LOOKING AT RECOVERY IN A NEW LIGHT

We need to see recovery from a new angle, one that's more inclusive and in-depth. We need to dig down deep, exploring the sources of our struggles. If we can work to destigmatize being in recovery, people struggling with addiction, mental health problems, and suicidal thoughts can come out of hiding and get the help they need.

My team at the Sober Truth Project primarily seeks to educate, empower, and advocate for two distinct groups:

1. *People in recovery* from addiction, mental health problems, and suicidal thoughts.

2. *People called to love and lead people in recovery* from addiction, mental health problems, and suicidal thoughts.

And believe it or not, most people find themselves in at least one if not both of these groups when a recovery touches their lives. When a colleague has a nervous breakdown. When a family member dies by suicide. When we come face-to-face with our own vices. It's only through these places of encounter that people develop a desire to go deeper and do more.

Recovery is for everyone. Because at its core, recovery is the gospel. You may never struggle with drug or alcohol addiction, anxiety or depression, or suicidal thoughts or ideation. But as a human, you probably *still* know what it's like to struggle—and you may be called to help the entire world learn to see recovery differently. Anything that replaces Jesus as Lord of your life, keeps you from your family and loved ones, and fills your life with disease (lack of ease) or hopelessness is your reason for recovery. And the reality is, all humans need recovery just like all sinners need a Savior.

COMMON STRUGGLES

Let's start by exploring three of humankind's most common struggles to uncover who recovery is truly meant for.

ADDICTION

Addictions don't always look the same. They can be chemical or behavioral, chosen or thrust upon you. Alcohol, drugs, sex, food, codependency, gambling, gaming, social media, shopping, offenses, exercise, politics—the list of potential addictions is endless. While struggling with sugar cravings might not seem to be as destructive as heroin or pornography, the neurological premise is the same.

MENTAL HEALTH

Mental health problems don't always look the same either; the tricky part is, they are often the underlying causes of addiction. These problems can include depression, anxiety, fear, attention deficit hyperactivity disorder, obsessive-compulsive disorder, post-traumatic stress disorder, bipolar disorder, perfectionism, oppositional defiance, eating disorders, borderline personality disorder, psychosis, schizophrenia, and more.

SUICIDAL THOUGHTS

Suicidal thoughts, tendencies, and ideation as well as other types of non-suicidal self-injury—such as cutting, self-mutilation, and other dissociative behavior—are technically mental health problems. However, they're so complex that it's helpful to place them into a separate category as people with no history of mental health problems can still experience them.

RECOVERY IS FOR EVERYONE

Maybe you saw yourself, a loved one, or someone you once loved in one of those descriptions. But whoever you are, wherever you're from, whatever life experiences you've had, I invite you to consider that maybe, *just maybe*, recovery is meant for you.

The Uncovery goes deep, unearthing not only surface-level struggles but identifying the root causes beneath the struggle. Trauma, stress, abuse, neglect, isolation, loneliness, discrimination, poverty, injury, job loss, unchecked power, homelessness, and physiological or neurological predisposition are all ways in which we come to the ends of ourselves, by choice or by chance. And they do not discriminate.

If recovery is the gospel, what does that look like? Jesus. It looks like Jesus.

Real recovery is good news that transforms hearts, minds, and lives. Real recovery brings lasting freedom, perpetual growth, wild discovery, heartfelt discipleship, and grace upon grace upon grace. Real recovery is a lifelong journey of discovery that reveals who we really are in Christ, who we always have been. The Uncovery looks like the unfathomably reckless love of God.

QUESTIONS FOR REFLECTION

1. What does the word "recovery" mean to you?

_____

_____

_____

_____

_____

2. How has your experience with traditional programming shaped your view of recovery?

_____

_____

_____

_____

_____

3. How does the statement, "Recovery is for everyone" make you feel and why?

_____

_____

_____

_____

_____

2

THE SPIRIT OF RECOVERY

But whenever anyone turns to the Lord,
the veil is taken away. Now the Lord is the Spirit, and where
the Spirit of the Lord is, there is freedom. And we all,
who with unveiled faces contemplate the Lord's glory, are
being transformed into his image with ever-increasing glory,
which comes from the Lord, who is the Spirit.
—2 Corinthians 3:16–18

Recovery is a journey, not a one-time event. It's never static, it's always moving, and it's rarely as stable and predictable as we'd like it to be.

The wildly unstable nature of recovery is perhaps the biggest problem we, the church, seem to have with it. We can't comprehend the scope of recovery, let alone predict it. And if we're honest, we'll admit that this scares us. We respond to that fear by trying to nail recovery down. We're quick to slap hurting people with a label, assimilate them into a program of the day, and pat ourselves on the backs for being such well-meaning saints. We then proceed to blame *them* when our one-size-fits-all solutions don't fit or work as we expected. In doing so, we miss out on countless opportunities to help people uncover their true identity in Christ, the identity of a beloved child of a good Father that's been available all along.

WE ARE THE CHURCH

Now, before I dig into a host of ways in which the church may be missing the boat when it comes to recovery, let me be very clear: when I say "we, the church," that includes me. Because we, the church of Jesus Christ, are supposed to be one. (See John 14:20; Galatians 3:28.) If I can't speak the word I'm about to lay down straight into the mirror, I have no authority to offer it to you in truth or in love. My goal with the Uncovery is simple: help uncover opportunities for the church of Jesus Christ to become who she is meant to be and who we were all created to be, together.

> TO LEARN HOW TO BE A HOSPITAL FOR SINNERS WHO NEED A SAVIOR INSTEAD OF AN ELITIST COUNTRY CLUB FOR SAINTS, WE NEED TO EMBRACE WHAT'S WORKING IN HOLY SPIRIT-LED RECOVERY.

If we, the church, are going to learn how to be a hospital for sinners who need a Savior instead of an elitist country club for saints, we need to embrace what's working—and let go of what's not working—in Holy Spirit-led recovery. I believe this will bring much-needed reform to the Christian church, not only for the obvious least of these, but for those of us who are hiding in plain sight. What's more, I believe the fruit of this reform will spill outside the walls of the church into our communities in a way that sparks revival and brings every last lost sheep home.

A growing number of Christians, especially those in the millennial generation and younger, are responding to traditional

Christian faith with a resounding, "You lost me."[4] We need to better understand the reasons why because they have a direct correlation to our impact potential in the recovery space. If the world sees churchgoing types as inauthentic, hypocritical, hypercritical, and untrustworthy, you'd better believe they won't be knocking on our doors for help in times of real crisis. When we start asking the *right* questions to get to the *real reasons* why there's a mass exodus from the Christian church, we can learn to more authentically love and lead people through any kind of recovery—straight to the *real* Jesus.

What if the revival we, the church, all want to see will require us to actually *be* the church? What if we broke down the manmade walls to be in the world, not of it? What if the church became a safe place for people to learn it's okay to admit you're not okay? What if people struggling with addiction, mental health problems, and suicidal thoughts weren't automatically viewed as "other," but were offered a relationship with God as Father? *What if?*

So here we go, church. Are we ready for a little tough love?

WE NEED TO LOVE, NOT ALIENATE

When it comes to helping people recover from addiction, mental health problems, and suicidal thoughts, we have work to do. Our often antiquated, legalistic mindsets can create stigmatizing and discriminatory barriers to entry for people from all walks of life who are really hurting. I dare say we're not doing it on purpose; it's just so deeply ingrained in our church cultures that we don't always realize it's happening. In an attempt to be the iron that sharpens iron (see Proverbs 27:17) and a shining example of healthy Christian boundaries, we have become better known by how we alienate, marginalize, and exclude than by our love.

---

4. "Six Reasons Young Christians Leave Church," Barna Group, September 27, 2011, www.barna.com/research/six-reasons-young-christians-leave-church.

Just ask my friend Shawn, a former urban church planter for a very well-known megachurch with prominent campuses across the nation. Although highly competent, energetic, and on fire for Jesus, Shawn was in recovery from years of struggle with bipolar disorder; a struggle he kept to himself. "Good pastors" like Shawn didn't struggle with things like mental illness. No, he was hired to help *other people* get free. So he left his issues at home, where he was conditioned throughout seminary and twelve years of full-time ministry to believe they belonged. He trained himself into a fake sense of *normalcy* in which he struggled to keep his secrets straight and became a different person in each group. Despite his real desire to be real with his peers, he hid, clinging to the anonymity and false certainty that comes with carefully prescribed and meticulously consumed medication.

> IN AN ATTEMPT TO BE A SHINING EXAMPLE OF HEALTHY CHRISTIAN BOUNDARIES, WE HAVE BECOME BETTER KNOWN BY HOW WE ALIENATE, MARGINALIZE, AND EXCLUDE THAN BY OUR LOVE.

Hiding in plain sight worked pretty well for Shawn—until it didn't. Six months into his assignment, due to pharmacy and insurance barriers beyond his control, he was unable to refill his bipolar medication prescription on the day he had to leave town for a two-week retreat with his ministry peers. Although the autonomous nature of his job allowed him keep multiple hospitalizations from his leadership team, Shawn knew calling off sick at the last minute for this reason would expose his mental health problems, damage his reputation, and jeopardize his position with the church. So despite the very real risks of withdrawal and relapse, he went.

Days into the retreat, the extreme pain of withdrawal from his medication caused his anxiety and paranoia to spike. Exhausted and overwhelmed, Shawn began to hear voices and hallucinate. He became fearful and highly suspicious of his peers, assuming they all knew exactly what was happening and were all against him. Shawn's downward spiral came to a head when he laid hands on a particularly high-challenge colleague—and not in a praying kind of way. Mortified, he fled the scene and hid out at home.

Days turned to weeks as the life Shawn had built came crashing down around him. His secret was finally out, and this uncalled-for outburst certainly wasn't how he'd hoped it would happen. Three years and $120,000 invested in seminary, with more than a decade of ministry, and it was all wasted in a heartbeat. He agonized over the call of God on his life that he now feared he would never be able to fulfill. Ultimately, Shawn stopped caring altogether. He slept the days away, wouldn't eat, avoided loved ones, and stopped taking care of himself. His wife recognized the clear warning signs of suicide. With a subtle sensitivity to the Spirit's leading, she gently and patiently led Shawn to choose another hospitalization over ending his life.

While under the hospital's care, Shawn's megachurch leaders and colleagues were strangely absent. No phone calls, texts, or emails were sent his family's way, but he learned plenty of disparaging, slanderous messages were sent to ministry partners across the nation about the incident. His identity shattered, Shawn knew his days in megachurches were numbered, but he still felt led to repent and attempt to reconcile with his team. What did he have to lose?

Back in a place of balance and health, Shawn and his wife reached out, united in their desire for reconciliation and peace with the church. But when Shawn made first contact with his superiors, they were, to put it kindly, less than grace-filled.

Instead of responding to his apology with love, support, or even prayer, Shawn was coldly notified of his termination. Leadership insisted his bipolar disorder was "no excuse" for his behavior; they maintained that he should have "disclosed" his issues early on so they might have avoided bringing someone so unstable into their leadership ranks. There was as little mercy for the incident as there was empathy for Shawn's need to hide in plain sight in the first place.

By the grace of God, Shawn has been able to rebuild a promised-land life and a powerful ministry with his wife. He believes his experiences have uniquely equipped him to love and lead the least of these at all levels. A plaque outside the door of their latest church plant reads "Judgment Free Zone," reminding Shawn and anyone else who crosses the threshold to live life out in the open—and stay open to the Holy Spirit's transformative power.

> THE STIGMATIZATION AND DISCRIMINATION AROUND MENTAL HEALTH PROBLEMS IN THE CHURCH ULTIMATELY CAUSE GOOD LEADERS WHO STRUGGLE TO HIDE—AND THEN FALL.

Shawn's story had a happy ending, but so many stories don't. The stigmatization and discrimination around mental health problems in the church ultimately cause good leaders who struggle to hide—and then fall. Hard. We see it all the time. And when our leaders fall, we, the church, are quick to cry out, *Hypocrite! Sinner! Wolf in sheep's clothing!* God forbid we would seek to restore them gently as Scripture asks of us. But if one of our perceived "best and brightest" like Shawn couldn't even find safe place in the church, someone like my friend Mike didn't have a prayer.

Mike came from a home as broken as they come, but stepped into an Italian-Catholic, extended-family existence where love meant being spoiled rotten and parental discipline was pretty much nonexistent. As a young man, Mike was searching for something. He didn't know he was looking for God. His experience with church was Mass on Christmas and Easter and a box-checking, right-of-passage confirmation process to ensure he could stay out of hell and be married one day. His ambition was obvious to all he knew, but Mike settled for money—*quick money*—to fill the God-shaped void in his heart. When academic and entrepreneurial pursuits fell through, Mike began selling marijuana, then cocaine, then sourcing and dealing even harder drugs until he found himself in and out of incarceration and supporting his own addictive habits.

When Mike's daughter was born, he hustled even harder, desperate to feed another mouth. When a severe overdose in 2008 left him in a life-threatening coma, her tiny voice whispering in the darkness, "Daddy, I need you" saved his life. To the shock of his care teams, Mike was awake and on his feet in a matter of weeks, learning how to walk, read, and do life all over again. Sober, restored, and highly motivated, Mike was released back into the world for a fresh start.

It only took four days of so-called freedom for Mike to relapse. Getting sober was a start, but he didn't yet have a life worth staying sober for. After six years of spiraling deeper into preexisting addictions, he finally lost custody of his daughter to the State of Florida in 2014.

Despite a life on the edge and little positive church experience, Mike always knew God was with him. Although his religious upbringing taught him the church was not a safe place to ask for help, he began to explore faith-based recovery programs in Tampa in 2015. While he found many churches chose to discriminate—or worse, assimilate—by process of elimination, Mike's exploration led him to my front door. Mike found his new home at the Timothy Initiative to be something entirely different. He was welcome, just as he was, for as long as he needed. He was surrounded by community, not for an hour a week or an intensive thirty-day detox, but to support him in every part of his life. He was valued for more than his sobriety; his whole life, his unfolding story, and his continued journey actually mattered. And above all, he was loved unconditionally by fellow broken men who became his brothers and by the Jesus he never knew before.

By the grace of God, Mike is now six years sober from drugs. It's a beautiful thing. But his sobriety is only the beginning. He regained full custody of his daughter and is now helping her raise his first grandchild. He married a wonderful woman who is also committed to a radical lifestyle of recovery. To this day, he and his family live on-site, and he serves as the director of recovery ministry for the Timothy Initiative, providing life resources and counseling to broken men. He has a call of God on his life to invite them into a promised-land life like the one he has built—and chooses to stay sober for every single day.

Shawn and Mike's stories can be painful to read, especially for recovery ministry leaders who want to provide a safe place to heal from addictions, mental health problems, and suicidal thoughts within the walls of the church. Believe me, I want that, too. And if I didn't believe for it, I wouldn't be able to invite the church to go deeper with me. But location may be the least of our worries at this point.

> MANY CHRISTIANS ARE MORE LIKELY TO LET PEOPLE BE DEFINED BY THEIR "SIN" RATHER THAN POINTING THEM TO THE SAVIOR WHO IS READY AND WILLING TO TRANSFORM THEIR LIVES.

The greatest challenges we face in Christian recovery are the implicit and explicit assumptions we have about addiction, mental health problems, and suicidal thoughts. Much of the church, believe it or not, holds fast to "sin" as the only culprit of any struggle. They're more likely to let people be defined by that sin rather than pointing them to Jesus, a Savior who is ready and willing to transform their lives.

IS ADDICTION A SIN PROBLEM?

When Jesus healed the man who was born blind, the disciples asked Him, "*Who sinned, this man or his parents?*" (John 9:2). Based on the Jewish teachings, they assumed his blindness was due to his sin or a generational curse. But Jesus corrected them: "*Neither this man nor his parents sinned…but this happened so that the works of God might be displayed in him*" (verse 3). The progressive healing left the man unrecognizable to his neighbors, who only knew him as a blind beggar.

If, like the disciples, you're still asking whether addiction, mental health problems, or suicidal thoughts are caused by personal sin, brought about by the sin actions of another, or just appear seemingly at random, you're asking the wrong questions. Statements like, "Hi, my name is George, and I'm an addict" becomes an identity people will cling to—and continue to sin into by faith. If all you believe you are is an addict, you'll continue to do what addicts do. The Uncovery resists calling out and clinging to sin with labels like "alcoholic," "schizophrenic," or "suicidal." It emphasizes people's righteousness in Christ and invites them to learn how to walk in it. The only identity label people in recovery need to embrace is "beloved child of God."

Addiction and compulsive behavior often stems from a loss of connection—from life and all it's meant to be filled with. Family and friends, passion and purpose, hope and a future. While the initial step away from a would-be promised-land life may come by way of personal sin, true separation takes two parties. Someone struggling with addiction may choose to use and disengage from people who would encourage sobriety. Someone struggling with mental health problems may hide and even disengage from the ones who love them most and would encourage therapy, medication, and self-care. Someone struggling with suicidal thoughts may never share them with anyone—until thoughts turn to tendencies, which turn into attempts on their own life. Those of us called to love and lead people to freedom in Christ as part of His body must be relentless in our pursuit of connection with the broken, the hurting, the angry, and the afraid. Our choice to throw our hands up in frustration and disengage can be as sinful as the actions that may have brought the individual to a place of suffering initially. If sin is the culprit, it's a sin we all commit.

> THOSE OF US CALLED TO LOVE AND LEAD PEOPLE TO FREEDOM IN CHRIST MUST BE RELENTLESS IN OUR PURSUIT OF CONNECTION WITH THE BROKEN, THE HURTING, THE ANGRY, AND THE AFRAID.

Even as I write this, I can already imagine your defense mechanisms rising about now. Before you rebut or dismiss my high-challenge stance, let me be clear: no one individual can be responsible for any other individual's recovery. I've tried it, and I've failed. Perhaps you have, too. But we, the church, can take *collective* responsibility for the pathways we create toward promised-land lives for people in recovery—if we can learn how to come together, as Jesus prayed we would.

> *I have given them the glory that you gave me, that they may be one as we are one—I in them and you in me—so that they may be brought to complete unity. Then the world will know that you sent me and have loved them even as you have loved me.*   (John 17:22–23)

What people in recovery need is a more empathetic, caring, and loving community. I believe we, the church, are uniquely positioned to be the solution and lead by example in this way.

It's not surprising that the "black hat, white hat," us vs. them mentality that permeates the church spills over into our Spirit-led recovery circles. Some traditions assume instantaneous supernatural healing from addiction and mental health problems…or bust. Others refuse to believe God still heals miraculously, especially in these areas. Some traditions dismiss almost any form of scientific breakthrough in diagnosis, treatment therapies, or medication; others assume issues like addiction and depression belong in physicians' offices, not prayer chains. Some traditions expect predictable, measurable results and uncompromising data to prove ministry effectiveness; to manipulate the numbers, some will even kick struggling brothers and sisters to the curb when relapse occurs. Some traditions require people to carry scarlet-letter labels for all to see even decades into sobriety; others fail to emphasize the importance of personal accountability and self-control in the recovery journey.

> HURTING PEOPLE HIDE BECAUSE WE, THE CHURCH, ARE FAILING TO CARRY OUT OUR CALL TO UNCONDITIONALLY LOVE AND LOOK AFTER THE LEAST OF THESE.

Friends, this is why people hide. This is why people disassociate. This is why people struggle to be vulnerable and honest. This is why people relapse—and why we, the church, are failing to carry out our call to unconditionally love and look after the least of these. Those who are sick. Those who are bound. Those hungry and thirsty for a drink of living water that really satisfies. Jesus makes His expectations clear. *"The King will reply, 'Truly I tell you, whatever you did for one of the least of these brothers and sisters of mine, you did for me*" (Matthew 25:40).

His next words in are some of the most sobering in all of Scripture.

> *Then he will say to those on his left, "Depart from me, you who are cursed, into the eternal fire prepared for the devil and his angels. For I was hungry and you gave me nothing to eat, I was thirsty and you gave me nothing to drink, I was a stranger and you did not invite me in, I needed clothes and you did not clothe me,* **I was sick and in prison and you did not look after me."** (Matthew 25:41–43)

Whatever we, the church, won't do for one of the least of these? We won't do it for Jesus either. People are sick, and people are in bondage. How they got there doesn't excuse us from setting both captives *and* prisoners free in the powerful name of Jesus. (See Isaiah 61:1; Romans 10:13.) If we won't come together to uncover the Spirit-led solutions right in front of us, one thing is certain— there will be eternal consequences.

RECOVERY IS THE GOSPEL

One of the more obvious reasons we, the church, need to reform Christian recovery is because it can be an undeniably powerful evangelistic tool. Recovery is for *everyone*, just as the gospel is for *everyone*. When Jesus died on the cross, He defeated sin once and *for all*. (See Romans 6:10.) When any of us believe we're not in need of recovery, we're essentially saying we're not in need of a Savior. We're rejecting God's gift of grace and His invitation to repent—which, by the way, simply means to change your mind. Yes, the good news of the gospel actually looks quite a bit like recovery. Saying "yes" to God's gift of grace and unmerited favor, turning away from our old ways of life, having a face-to-face encounter with the Father, and choosing to keep our eyes locked on Jesus on a journey of discovery that leads to a promised-land life. This radical grace gift isn't reserved for sanctimonious saints or puritanical perfectionists—it's for broken men and women just like you and me. Recovery is the gospel.

When my friend Mac was injured in a Navy SEAL Team 6 exercise, he was left with brain damage that caused severe PTSD. After a lifetime of uncharacteristically high achievement, elite recognition, and great privilege, he struggled to see himself outside of his high-ranking military identity. Several well-meaning counselors and recovery specialists came to see Mac, but he resented their charity-case mentalities and constant labeling. Words like "disabled," "damaged," and "handicapped" did not go over well with Mac. He tried turning to the church for help, but he found the leaders more interested in shaming sinners into repentance than introducing them to a Savior. Five minutes into his first men's meeting, a fellow former soldier struggling with PTSD accidentally said the word "shit" when describing a traumatic experience—and the rest of the meeting was spent addressing his foul language instead of his trauma. Defeated and disgusted, Mac isolated himself, which made his mental health problems even worse.

The first time I met Mac, he wasn't quick to open up. Digging deep into the Uncovery is much harder when the ground is still frozen. So I came with no agenda or expectations of Mac beyond sitting and spending time with him and just...*listening*. It didn't take long for Mac to realize I didn't see him as a pet project or a problem to fix. I saw him as a regular guy in need of a friend. More than that, I saw him as a man who was always meant to be my brother, not just my ministry success story. Initiating with authenticity, grace, and love in this way opened the door to fruitful conversations about recovery and about Jesus—someone Mac never knew he needed until every piece of his false identity was stripped away.

Did God cause Mac's accident to draw him closer? Of course not! It's not in God's character to bring harm to the ones He loves, the ones Jesus died to save. He doesn't leave ninety-nine sheep to go after the lost one, only to slaughter him! No, the Good Shepherd didn't cause Mac's accident, but He did use it to bring Mac into my life and start an Uncovery journey that's leading to a promised-land life. Even better, God is still using Mac's story to help me spread the gospel and inspire unity in the body of Christ.

> WE, THE CHURCH, ARE CAUSING OUR BROTHERS AND SISTERS TO STRAIGHT-UP SIN BECAUSE WE HAVE MORE FAITH IN THEIR ABILITY TO SIN THAN IN GOD'S ABILITY TO HEAL.

Mac and countless other people who have experienced physical, emotional, or psychological trauma find themselves in need of recovery. They didn't ask for their current disorder, they didn't want it, and, in many cases, they did nothing to contribute to it. They are operating as a product of it, not the cause of it. We, the church, have failed to recognize this, and we are causing our brothers and sisters to not only stumble, but to straight-up sin because we have more faith in their ability to sin than in God's ability to heal. If we don't begin to go deeper into the Uncovery, taking into consideration the whole-life experience, we will be setting future generations up to deal with the same problems we're facing today.

The scientific community has done a fantastic job of identifying common pathways into addiction. For example, the Adverse Childhood Experiences (ACE) Study shows how childhood trauma plays a role in addiction, mental health problems, and suicide.[5] Generational trauma exists because people have always been unable or unwilling to name what was wrong. Now we know better. The evidence is all around us. And yet, the Christian community stays painfully silent on what the rest of the world might call social justice issues.

We, the church, need to take responsibility for our youth, not only through practical checks and balances systems to keep them safe, but through fervent prayer and advocacy for the well-being of future generations. And when one little lamb goes missing, we mustn't blame the lamb. We must go after him, risking everything to bring him home again—to a safer flock than the one he left.

> *If anyone causes one of these little ones—those who believe in me—to stumble, it would be better for them to have a large millstone hung around their neck and to be drowned in the depths of the sea. Woe to the world because of the things that cause people to stumble! Such things must come, but woe to the person through whom they come!* (Matthew 18:6–7)

Beyond loving and leading our little ones well, we, the church, must be willing to embrace trauma-informed ministry on a much deeper level. Getting free is only half the battle. Knowing what ensnared you in the first place empowers a promised-land life—not only for people who struggle, but for future generations that may never need to struggle if we act now. We won't walk this out perfectly. But together, we can make a measurable difference in the lives of people currently in recovery and those who could be one day. Perhaps that will be you, your children, your children's children, or your friend, neighbor, or loved one, each one a beloved child of God who deserves better than the lie of a label.

---

5. Vincent J. Felitti, "The Relation Between Adverse Childhood Experiences and Adult Health: Turning Gold into Lead," *The Permanente Journal*, Winter 2002, www.ncbi.nlm.nih.gov/pmc/articles/PMC6220625.

DON'T BE *OF* THIS WORLD, BUT DO BE *IN* IT

I believe one of the greatest opportunities for the advancement of the gospel in recovery circles actually exists *outside* the walls of the church. As chosen, set-apart believers, we know we're meant to be in the world, not of it. (See John 17:14–19.) Sadly, we, the church, use this as an excuse to segregate ourselves from people groups who don't look, think, act, live, and believe like we do—or at least like we think they should. When we do this, we miss key revelation intelligence the Father has strategically placed in the hearts and minds of would-be believers who haven't met the real Jesus yet. He's hidden gold in their hearts for us to uncover and use for our good and His glory. And if people outside the walls of the church don't know what they carry, guess what? It's on us.

> EVEN SECULAR MENTAL HEALTH PROFESSIONALS BELIEVE FAITH PLAYS A KEY ROLE IN RECOVERY.

The wild thing is, the nonspiritual recovery world isn't as against us as we, the church, might be tempted to believe. Even secular mental health professionals believe faith plays a key role in recovery. A 2019 report from the *Journal of Religion and Health* made it plain:

> We conclude that the value of faith-oriented approaches to substance abuse prevention and recovery is indisputable. And, by extension, we also conclude that the decline in religious affiliation in the USA is not only a concern for religious organizations but constitutes *a national health concern.*[6]

6. Brian J. Grim and Melissa E. Grim, "Belief, Behavior, and Belonging: How Faith is Indispensable in Preventing and Recovering from Substance Abuse," *Journal of Religion and Health*, July 29, 2019, www.ncbi.nlm.nih.gov/pmc/articles/PMC6759672.

Did you catch that? Even *science* thinks there's value to Spirit-led recovery! But the reality is, science has little to lose by operating autonomously in a secular world. We, the church, however, have everything to lose—lives and souls at stake. That's why it's our responsibility to extend the olive branch. We must create and invite secular psychologists, counselors, and mental health professionals into safe places for sharing knowledge, co-laboring as partners, and facilitating honest discussions with no agenda beyond going deeper together. The Holy Spirit will convict and call hearts and minds on His own terms—we're off the hook.

God loves to show Himself in scientific and medical breakthroughs in the same way He reveals Himself in the glory of His creation. Imagine what the spiritual community and the scientific community stand to learn from one another...if we would only come together.

ELEVATING THE RECOVERY CONVERSATION

When Jesus walked the earth, He brought hope, healing, and salvation to people's houses. What He didn't bring was a list of go-to behavior modification strategies. More often than not in Scripture, we catch a glimpse of Jesus doing healing and initial deliverance, but we don't always know what happened next. I believe these are divine omissions, places where we, the church, are meant to rise up and assume responsibility for the people God has set free from sin. It's in these uncertain places that we're meant to seek God's wisdom, both personally and corporately, about the church's continued role in recovery, which goes beyond supporting sobriety into Uncovery territory.

Even taking all of Scripture into context, none of us knows exactly what that looks like. *"We know in part and we prophesy in part"* (1 Corinthians 13:9), so none of us have all the answers. I know I don't. But I do know this: transformation can only be birthed out of authentic, loving relationships. It's possible to be so right you're actually wrong in the unloving way you speak truth. What's more, the truths we cling to can and will continually be reformed and refined by God Himself. Have you ever met someone whose spiritual walk with Jesus never required a single round of theological tweaking or loving correction from the Father? Me either.

THE UNCOVERY: A THREE-PART FRAMEWORK

Venturing into Uncovery territory requires a genuine encounter with a loving heavenly Father. The most effective way we, the church, can represent the Father well is to represent Jesus well in our interactions—to initiate with grace and love instead of judgment and condemnation. This part of the Uncovery requires three unique behaviors of us—and as you might have guessed by now, you will struggle to find them in even the very best of twelve-step programs.

1. ASK THE RIGHT QUESTIONS

"How do we get people sober?" certainly isn't a *bad* question—and most leaders who ask it are genuine. But if we want to lead people into life transformation, the question we need to ask is, "Why are they bound in the first place?" People struggling with addiction, mental health problems, and suicidal thoughts will usually tell us exactly how they ended up there if we're willing to ask the right questions and listen more than we talk. When we better understand the origin of their struggles, we can better understand how to show compassion and help them build a promised-land life worth staying sober for. What's more, we can identify systemic change opportunities to prevent future generations from falling into the same traps.

2. LISTEN TO THE HOLY SPIRIT

When you're privileged enough to speak one-on-one with someone who is struggling, keep one ear on them and one ear tuned in to the Holy Spirit. Be humble, gentle, and empathetic, remembering you are just a fellow traveler on a journey toward a promised-land life. I'm convinced that any one of us is only two or three choices away from a life of complete self-destruction, which is why I believe recovery is for everyone. Even if you are in a place of transformational victory and are certain you have all the answers that someone is seeking, wait for the Spirit's prompting before you offer up any solutions. If you speak out of turn without the Spirit's gentle nudge, they will hear your condemnation, not the Spirit's conviction. When that happens, you may lose them altogether.

3. HELP TO IDENTIFY THE RIGHT NEXT STEPS

Even the most transformative meetings, counseling sessions, and conversations can be less than helpful when you, the fellow traveler, go missing on the journey. While you may not be called to walk with an individual throughout their entire life's journey, God will ask you to be available for more than a one-time talk. Sponsors and accountability partners are a great start. But what happens when they can't answer a call or drop everything to come running in a moment of need? People in recovery need real relationships with real people—and they need more than one accountability partner. But the issue is about more than mere availability. There may be times when you realize that you aren't the person to journey with them, especially when gender or competing issues might get in the way. A man in recovery from sexual addiction should not lean on a woman with codependency issues. A woman working through her husband's infidelity should not lean on a male single pastor. The bottom line is that it does take a village. And we know this because we were created for relationship.

THE THREE-PART UNCOVERY FRAMEWORK REQUIRES A WILLINGNESS TO DIVE BENEATH THE SUPERFICIAL SURFACE ISSUES INTO THE ROOT CAUSE OF A PERSON'S BROKENNESS.

This three-part Uncovery framework may be simple, but it's certainly not easy. It requires a willingness to dive beneath the superficial surface issues into the root cause of a person's brokenness. When we commit to going beyond twelve steps by asking the right questions, listening to the Holy Spirit, and helping to identify the right next steps, the Holy Spirit is more than capable of leading people to adjust any viewpoints they're clinging to that are inconsistent with God's truth. Friends, we can't bully anyone to the cross! But we can put the Jesus in us on display by showing up for people as He would—by demonstrating love, respect, empathy, and devotion, all covered in equal parts truth and grace.

SEEKING A LIFE TRANSFORMATION

The ultimate goal for people in recovery is not sobriety. Just as the moment of getting saved is only the start of spiritual growth and maturity, getting sober is only the beginning of the recovery journey. It's not about numbers; it's about total life transformation. The true purpose of Spirit-led recovery is to lead people into a promised-land life worth staying sober for. As you may have already guessed, I don't believe this transformation is possible but for the grace of God through His Son, Jesus. This is why I've dedicated my life to serving, honoring, and reinstating broken men and women, some of whom have been hurt by the church, inviting them to be part of a radical community life. I've tasted and seen that the Lord is good (see Psalm 34:8) as He has poured grace upon grace into people's lives, reconciling the world back to Himself because of His wild and reckless love for them. We, the church, are meant to be conduits of this grace.

You may not be called to a radical lifestyle of community. That's okay. You may not be called to break a faithfully established boundary to be the one to initiate with grace. That's okay. You may not be personally called to bridge the gap between Spirit and science by engaging with medical professionals. That's okay, too.

But you can still support going beyond twelve steps by refusing to stigmatize and discriminate in and out of the church. You can still choose to forgive people whose addictions and mental health problems have caused you harm. You can still refuse to balk when you hear of medical breakthrough in recovery circles, keeping your heart and mind open to however God chooses to reveal His truth. You can still choose to honor the divine DNA in all people, regardless of whether they look, act, think, vote, believe, or behave like you do—or like you think they should.

You can do this. And if you still don't think you can, remember, recovery is for you, too.

QUESTIONS FOR REFLECTION

1. What do you think it means to be in the world but not of it?

_____

_____

_____

_____

_____

2. Have you witnessed or participated in stigmatization and/or discrimination against people in recovery? Describe your experience.

_____

_____

_____

_____

_____

3. Which part of the Uncovery's three-part framework challenges you the most:

+ Ask the right questions

+ Listen to the Holy Spirit

+ Help to identify the right next steps

_____

_____

_____

_____

_____

3

THE SCIENCE OF RECOVERY

Sometimes you can only find heaven by
slowly backing away from hell.
—Carrie Fisher

The woman whose story is told in Matthew 9:20–22, Mark 5:25–
34, and Luke 8:43–48 had been bleeding out for twelve long, painful years. It's no wonder she was so desperate to get to Jesus. She
knew if she could only touch the edge of his cloak, she would be
healed, so she pressed through the crowd to reach Him. Her faith
motivated her boldness and healed her—to her delight and Jesus's
glory.

The Bible doesn't explain how or why this woman was con-
stantly bleeding. Maybe a horrible accident left her that way.
Maybe she was hormonally imbalanced, diseased, cursed, pos-
sessed, or addicted. Maybe she was suffering in the aftermath of
horrific trauma or ongoing violent abuse. We can't know for sure.
There was no documented medical diagnosis, only the original
Greek word *haemorrhoissa* or "bleeding woman," which would
have left her with nasty labels like "unclean" and "unwelcome" in
both social and religious circles under Jewish law. This woman
"had suffered a great deal under the care of many doctors and had

spent all she had, yet instead of getting better she grew worse" (Mark 5:26). No matter what the cause of her problem, she knew Jesus as Jehovah-Rapha—the Lord Who Heals. She knew one touch would be enough for her.

The irony is that this bleeding woman couldn't have picked a worse time to interrupt Jesus's day. Surrounded by an entourage of disciples and a crowd of spectators, He was walking across town with a prominent Jewish leader named Jairus, whose twelve-year-old daughter was dead or dying. (See Matthew 9:18–19, Mark 5:22–24, Luke 8:41–42.) We don't know how or why this little girl came face-to-face with death, but we do know that like the bleeding woman, Jairus had faith that Jesus could heal and bring his daughter back to life.

When we compare the two situations, we might quickly conclude that the twelve-year-old girl's death was far more pressing than the woman who had been bleeding out for twelve years. Jesus certainly couldn't heal everybody, so he probably had to prioritize, right?

Imagine how exasperated Jairus, the disciples, and the crowd must've been when Jesus stopped cold en route to resurrecting the little girl to say, *"Who touched me?…Someone touched me; I know that power has gone out from me"* (Luke 8:45, 46).

They might have thought, *Come on now, Jesus, a kid's life is hanging in the balance! We don't have time for this! Let's go!*

And this bleeding woman was probably pretty nervous because *"seeing that she could not go unnoticed, [she] came trembling and fell at his feet"* (Luke 8:47).

How many times have people come to the church for help only to be shamed for far less than they came for? Lucky for the bleeding woman, Jesus wasn't in a hurry. He stopped, turned around, and looked right at her. Face-to-face with that gaze of reckless grace, the woman heard the words every single person who struggles with addiction, mental health, and suicidal thoughts wants to hear. Jesus said, *"Daughter, your faith has healed you. Go in peace"* (Luke 8:48).

If you've heard this story before, you know it gets even better. After Jesus leaves the faith-filled woman who's been healed, he gets to Jairus's house, where family and friends have already started to mourn and play a funeral dirge for the little girl.

> *"Stop wailing," Jesus said. "She is not dead but asleep." They laughed at him, knowing that she was dead. But he took her by the hand and said, "My child, get up!" Her spirit returned, and at once she stood up.*   (Luke 8:52–55)

TWO RELATED MIRACLES

This intertwined narrative is as true as it is symbolic. The little girl represents Israel, God's chosen people—who are not dead, but asleep—coming alive in the truth about their identity. The bleeding woman represents the church—a bride in need of reform and ready for the Bridegroom—healed and restored to purity on the way to a resurrection of all God's people. Twelve years—the girl's age and the length of the woman's suffering—represents earthly authority and divine perfection that can only come from God. Twelve is the product of three, which denotes the divine, and four, which represents the earth or creation. Thus this story of the dying girl and the bleeding woman brings heaven and earth together in two separate but related miracles.

Jesus is Jehovah-Rapha, our Healer, whether we choose to believe it or not. And He will bring healing and deliverance however and whenever He chooses. Jesus is coming back for us. I believe that even now, the Father is healing the church in a move that will spark revival and redemption in the secular world if we, the church, would have even a tassel's touch of faith.

When twelve years can be transformed in a moment, it's hard to accept lifelong suffering. My friend Maria struggled with addiction and mental health problems since she was in her twenties. She spent most of her life in and out of psychiatric lockdown facilities. She'd been through every psychological, consultive, medicinal, and therapeutic means of treatment you could imagine—including shock therapy and other wildly controversial regimens. They didn't help her maintain sobriety or regain her mental clarity, but they did quite possibly make things worse through the years. The medical community gave Maria the labels "addict" and "psychotic," and she believed them. They assumed that she, like the bleeding woman, was in a perpetual state of uncleanliness and needed to be sheltered away from authentic community. To them, Maria was a problem that couldn't be solved.

Julie and I met Maria when she was in her early fifties and welcomed her without question into our community. While in a safe place with us, she met the real Jesus and was introduced to a heavenly Father who loved her unconditionally and called her His daughter whether she felt and acted like it or not. Even in sober living, she continued to struggle with addiction and mental health. But for the first time ever, she had a peace about who she really was underneath her struggles. She wanted to be *that* Maria.

Ten years into our relationship, Maria died tragically before ever reaching the promised-land life we tried so hard to help her build. No matter how many success stories we have through the Timothy Initiative, the Just Initiative, and the Sober Truth Project, my heart breaks and aches for the ones who, by worldly definition, "fail out." As Julie and I spent time with Maria's family to mourn the loss of our beloved sister, I couldn't shake the guilt over my inability to save her. We had been willing, and we all went all in. But we still lost her. I imagined her family would be disappointed not only in my methods, but also in me.

By grace alone, Maria's family shared a very different story. They described overwhelming relief—even joy—that Maria was no longer struggling or in pain. They told us that after a lifetime of failure and exclusion, she had finally made her way home into a community of people who helped her understand that she would never be perfect this side of heaven—and that was okay. They said the peace Maria felt and lived out in her last ten years of life were more than they could have ever dreamed of for her. Even in death, Maria knew she was worthy of love and that her life had eternal significance. "You didn't just save her life, you saved her soul," they insisted. "We are so thankful."

You might be tempted to believe that the scientific community failed Maria. Please don't. As human beings, we only know what we know when we know it. This is true when it comes to medical breakthrough and spiritual breakthrough. I believe science was created *by* God and brings glory *to* God. Science continues to prove the existence of absolute truth in the same way Scripture continues to prove the true nature of God. The scientific community is always going deeper, learning new things all the time. And if we, the church, followed suit, we could be doing the same.

> SCIENCE CONTINUES TO PROVE THE EXISTENCE OF ABSOLUTE TRUTH IN THE SAME WAY SCRIPTURE CONTINUES TO PROVE THE TRUE NATURE OF GOD.

While medical professionals used to assume diagnoses were permanent, experimental therapies were acceptable, and isolating struggling humans was a right and reasonable course of action, they now know better. Every day, neuroscientists are losing labels and embracing epigenetics, a science that focuses on how life experiences influence gene function, as they learn more about the brain's ability to heal itself. Every day, therapists are examining age-old methods more deeply to preserve patient dignity. Every day, mental health professionals are discovering just how much people need people—that we are somehow *meant* to thrive in community. These breakthroughs are nothing short of miraculous, and God's hand is guiding this revelation as He continues to reconcile the world to Himself.

While we, the church, used to persecute and even murder nonbelievers, water down the gospel to make it more palatable (and lucrative by proxy), and excommunicate instead of loving the least of these, we also now know better. It's probably why you're reading this book. Every day, we have new opportunities to love our neighbors as ourselves. Every day, we have new opportunities to learn more about God as Father as His Spirit speaks through His Word. Every day, we have new opportunities to be known as Christians by our love for practitioners and patients alike.

Dr. Amir Aczel, an Israeli-born American author and lecturer in mathematics and science, once famously refuted "new atheist" claims that religion and science are mutually exclusive:

> The deeper we delve into the mysteries of physics and cosmology, the more the universe appears to be intricate and incredibly complex. To explain the quantum-mechanical behavior of even one tiny particle requires pages and pages of extremely advanced mathematics. Why are even the tiniest particles of matter so unbelievably complicated? It appears that there is a vast, hidden "wisdom," or structure, or knotty blueprint for even the most simple-looking element of nature...Science and religion are two sides of the same deep human impulse to understand the world, to know our place in it, and to marvel at the wonder of life and the infinite cosmos we are surrounded by. Let's keep

them that way, and not let one attempt to usurp the role of the other.[7]

The Uncovery requires growth and change—learning, unlearning, and relearning the truth about who we were created to be. Even with the best of intentions, most professional relationships alone cannot offer a comprehensive and authentic version of love's attributes—validation, acceptance, worth, belonging, and significance—and not just because most professionals are paid to care. Overwhelmed schedules can result in data-driven dehumanizing, over- and under-medicating, and recovery leaders hiding their own addiction and mental health struggles in plain sight. Yes, professional relationships will rightly require some hard-and-fast healthy boundaries. That's where personal, Spirit-filled relationships can often pick up where science leaves off. Scientific professionals need and want the church to step up in this way— because just like us, they alone can't be solely responsible for someone's recovery.

BRIDGING THE GAP

Whether a struggling person's issue is physical, spiritual, or a mix of the two, we, the church, are uniquely suited to bridge the gap between Spirit and science by:

+ Co-laboring with professionals to whom God chooses to bring breakthrough
+ Loving those professionals just as much as we love their patients

Dr. Amanda Gene Sharp, co-founder of the Sober Truth Project, wrote her dissertation on the role of non-secular involvement toward a comprehensive community approach for addressing opioid use disorder. Amanda is an agnostic research assistant and

---

7. Amir D. Aczel, "Why Science Does Not Disprove God," *TIME* magazine, April 27, 2014, time.com/77676/why-science-does-not-disprove-god.

post-doctoral fellow with Harvard University's Cambridge Health Alliance and the University of South Florida. She insists that there's an intrinsic value to faith-based and spiritual organizations' involvement in recovery—so long as they're not too caught up in legalistic *religiosity*. Amanda says the faith element in recovery is a key benefit to the struggling individual and the community at large.

Her 2020 dissertation speaks volumes to the value of partnering with secular professionals in the recovery process:

> A partnership between faith-based organizations (FBOs) and behavioral health entities that leverages the network potential of religious social capital is one such collaboration that could effectively bridge gaps towards the delivery of comprehensive solutions for individuals suffering from an OUD [opioid use disorder].[8]

But it's not just the secular philosophical community that sees the value of faith-based recovery. Alternative medicine advocates like Deepak Chopra and neurosurgeons like Dr. Sanjay Gupta also insist that the faith element is key. Their collaborative work has proven the brain's ability to heal itself from the damages of addiction and the power of visualization to turn abstract hopes and dreams into a promised-land life that "not only inspires you, but also guides you."[9]

With all due respect, I believe my contemporaries working in behavioral health, medicine, or neurological research are trying to measure the immeasurable. Ironically, I believe many of the

---

8. A. G. Sharp, *The Role of Non-Secular Involvement Towards a Comprehensive Community Approach for Addressing Opioid Use Disorder*, 2020 doctoral dissertation, University of South Florida.
9. Kabir Sehgal and Deepak Chopra, "Do this for 5 minutes every day to rewire your brain for success, according to neuroscience," CNBC, April 5, 2019, www.cnbc.com/2019/04/03/deepak-chopra-sanjay-gupta-simple-trick-to-training-your-brain-for-success-according-to-neuroscience.html.

theories they posit point straight toward a much-needed relationship with our good Father God. This relationship element becomes especially important when walking alongside a person in recovery through the wilderness. And perhaps even more so as we, the church, learn what it really looks like to unify and operationalize the idea of the Uncovery, transcending all kinds of theological, denominational, and religious strongholds.

Even after facing the most severe consequences, people in recovery from addiction, mental health problems, and suicidal thoughts still struggle and relapse. It's not because they're "doing it wrong." It's because sometimes the brain doesn't heal in lockstep with the heart. You can be a rescued, redeemed, and blood-bought believer in Jesus and still struggle. It's one of the most profound mysteries we humans face, and yet it's no surprise to God. His inconceivable strength, after all, is made perfect in our weakness. (See 2 Corinthians 12:9.)

> EVEN AFTER FACING THE MOST SEVERE CONSEQUENCES, PEOPLE IN RECOVERY STILL STRUGGLE AND RELAPSE BECAUSE THE BRAIN DOESN'T ALWAYS HEAL IN LOCKSTEP WITH THE HEART.

KNOW YOUR BRAIN BASICS

Before you dismiss what science can bring to the table in Christian recovery, it's important to educate yourself on how the brain works. If you've seen people fall back into addiction, mental health problems, and suicidal thoughts even after faithful interventions and very real consequences, you may be ready to go deeper into the science of behavior and why we can't judge a person's recovery journey based on behavior alone.

Now, I'm not a doctor. I've never been medically trained, and I'm certainly unqualified to lead any sort of clinical team. But my interactions with the scientific community have given me some understanding of the depth and breadth of damage that can be reversed in a person's recovery. For instance, in the case of addiction, "abstinence from drugs and alcohol for a year or longer has been shown to allow the brain to begin repairing structural damage caused by drug toxicity, which in turn improves cognitive function and allows chemically dependent patients to exert stronger self-control."[10]

Epigenetic studies have already proven that there is no addiction gene.[11] Addiction is a product of early-childhood environmental factors, not genetic predisposition. A lack of prenatal and postnatal nurturing can cause certain genes to go dormant, making excessive consumption and addiction more likely. These dormant genes, through trauma-informed care, can be awakened once again to combat addictive tendencies! These types of breakthroughs have fostered better patient care for individuals who would have once labeled "generational addicts" because of their family origins. Discoveries such as these should foster compassion and grace for each person's unique recovery journey, including our own. What's more, it encourages opportunities for kinship collaboration with medical professionals who need community and practical support in leading reform.

The brain is a miraculous thing. It's a wonder to me that anyone could consider this three-pound, highly adaptive organ with a hundred billion neurons and not see the fingerprint of God on each person. The brain can't feel pain, but it can be damaged. The tiniest chemical shift in serotonin can cause a splitting headache. Add in stress, trauma, disease, disorders, and non-organic chemical

---

10. "Drug Abuse, Dopamine, and the Brain's Reward System," Butler Center for Research, September 1, 2015, www.hazeldenbettyford.org/education/bcr/addiction-research/drug-abuse-brain-ru-915.
11. Maia Szalavitz, "Genetics: No more addictive personality," *Nature*, June 24, 2015, www.nature.com/articles/522S48a.

compounds like drugs and alcohol, and the brain's neurotransmitters and neurological pathways can become quite literally *rewired*, causing long-term reduced cognitive function.[12] The brain's ability to adapt and change like this, for better or for worse, is known as neuroplasticity. The longer the addiction, mental health problem, or suicidal thoughts continue, the more deeply ingrained they can become, making traditional recovery far more difficult.

By the grace of God, medical research has proven that the human brain has the ability to rewire its own neurological pathways. Yes, the brain can actually unlearn addictive, disordered behavior and reset itself. Mindfulness and meditation have been proven to help reduce the risk of relapse, which can be a permanent struggle even for people back in a place of health.[13] And new studies of the structural changes that occur in an addicted brain are even now helping scientists and medical professionals develop new treatments, medications, and therapies. Acknowledging and celebrating these breakthroughs does no harm to the Christian church.

Embracing what the scientific community brings to the table will only help people achieve an unprecedented level of healing. What if a former heroin addict needs lofexidine to help him cope and build a promised-land life? What if someone who struggles with bipolar disorder needs lamotrigine to help her stay balanced and whole? What if someone struggling with suicidal thoughts needed therapy and antidepressants to see they have a life that's worth living? God moves in mysterious ways. And we, the church, certainly don't want to miss what He's doing in the scientific community.

---

12. "Drugs, Brains, and Behavior: The Science of Addiction," National Institute on Drug Abuse, NIH Pub No. 14-5605, nida.nih.gov/sites/default/files/soa_2014.pdf.
13. Katie Witkiewitz et al., "Retraining the addicted brain: A review of hypothesized neurobiological mechanisms of mindfulness-based relapse prevention," *Psychology of Addictive Behaviors*, June 2013, pubmed.ncbi.nlm.nih.gov/22775773.

It really is okay to have Jesus *and* a therapist—and we, the church, need to make sure people know it.

IT'S ALL ABOUT RELATIONSHIP

Whether you're working toward your own promised-land life, helping others build one, or both, the Uncovery is about one thing. It's not about the journey or the destination. It's about the company you keep.

It's important to stay present in the moment, tuned into what God is doing in you and through you as well as in and through the people around you. The best way you can do this is to surround yourself with a community of people who want the same thing you do—to see a full-on reformation in the recovery space that breaks the chains of addiction for future generations. Notice I didn't say people who look like you, think like you, act like you, worship like you, love like you, vote like you, or live like you. Nope. While there's nothing wrong with having friends who fit your mold, being like-minded in these ways can do more harm than good when you're pushing for positive change.

We need to learn what it means to love our enemies, honor them through disagreement, and lean in hard to honor what they bring to the table. We need to honor people trying to love and lead in recovery, despite denominational, religious, and cultural differences. The keys to breakthrough in the recovery space are buried in the hearts and minds of those whom we, the church, might be tempted to keep at a distance. Coming together to care by fostering authentic and safe relationships with them is our only hope of bridging the gap.

THE KEYS TO BREAKTHROUGH IN THE RECOVERY SPACE ARE BURIED IN THE HEARTS AND MINDS OF THOSE WHOM WE, THE CHURCH, MIGHT BE TEMPTED TO KEEP AT A DISTANCE.

You may be asking, "How do we engage in a conversation like that with a medical doctor who rejects Jesus? With a dry drunk more addicted to meetings than anything else? With a family that's lost everything, including relationships, marriages, and even loved ones' lives?" The answer is simple, but it's not easy. With humility. You can position your heart to learn all you can. You can ask open-ended questions and resist the urge to fix, correct, or brag. You can offer insight, perspective, support, and love where you can. You can invite others to offer insight, perspective, support, and love where they can. By all means, be honest and unapologetic about your own beliefs and mission. But lay your agenda aside and treat your potential co-laborers as the beloved children of God they are—even if they don't know it yet. Only through authentic and safe relationships like these can real breakthrough come. And only in this way could we ever hope for the opportunity to share the truth about the hope we have in God.

LOVING AND LEADING IN RECOVERY

We, the church, can speak even greater volumes by the unusual way we love and lead people in Christian recovery. It starts with making sure people know they belong before they even believe. From a practical application standpoint, this means empowering people to lead who might never be asked otherwise.

It might mean dropping every label that creates a barrier to people coming together.

It might mean rebuking discrimination against people in recovery.

It might mean second chances.

And third chances.

And seventh chances.

And seventy-seventh chances.

It might mean loving as radically and inclusively as Jesus does.

If the world sees the church as a bigoted, hypocritical, and hypercritical country club, only we, the church, can change their minds. It's time for us to rise up and be the bride of Christ we were always meant to be. Let's be the ones to bridge the gap between Spirit and science in Jesus's name. May the words of Jesus to Jairus's daughter ring true for us today. "Wake up! You're not dead; you're only sleeping!"

And when we do wake up? I believe we'll see people coming to Christ like we've never witnessed before. God will heal the *whole church* en route to reconciling the *whole world* to Himself.

QUESTIONS FOR REFLECTION

1. How did the intertwined narrative of the bleeding woman and Jairus's daughter speak to you?

_____

_____

_____

_____

_____

2. How have you handled not seeing the miracles you wanted to see in recovery?

_____

_____

_____

_____

3. What do we stand to gain by bridging the gap between Spirit and science in Christian recovery?

_____

_____

_____

_____

PART II

RELEARNING RECOVERY

Even in what seems like total randomness, there is order. Chaotic, complex systems are at play in every facet of creation and every fiber of our beings, pointing to an all-seeing, all-knowing, all-powerful Father God—a God who gives us free will and still chooses to redeem the stories we try to write apart from Him and in spite of His goodness. He honors even the slightest repentance and empowers our *"faith as small as a mustard seed"* (Matthew 17:20) to move mountains and bring His kingdom.

God isn't looking for another recovery program. He doesn't need another surefire system, another plug-and-play counseling series, or another cutting-edge curriculum. He wants a mindset shift in His church. Big or small, personal or corporate, God is renewing the hearts and minds of people struggling with or leading people through addiction, mental health problems, and suicidal thoughts—and preemptively healing generations that will one day be born into an abundant, promised-land life. And you, my friend, are being invited to participate in this unprecedented shifting. Are you ready?

4

RETHINKING RELAPSE

It's never about the dishes.
—George Wood

Doing life in a sober-living community like the one we've built within the Timothy Initiative is not without its challenges. Like other recovery communities, we have house rules, clear expectations, and community guidelines to help us cooperate, co-labor, and thrive. While we aren't too quick to excommunicate someone when these rules are violated, we never ignore a breach in protocol—and there's an important reason why. When even a simple breakdown in the community lifestyle happens, it's typically a sign of a much bigger problem.

Oftentimes, the guys will come to me to vent about how someone isn't pulling his weight, saying things like, "He's slacking off at work," "He's always missing curfew," or "He never helps with the dishes!" The list of grievances goes on. When our men are working diligently to comply with community guidelines, it can feel like a slight when their fellow T.I. brothers aren't doing the same.

Now, I care about how our collective community feels. Our other leaders do, too. We're in extremely close quarters, and there is bound to be some interpersonal conflict. But the primary reason I care about these breaches in conduct is because they typically happen just before someone relapses. So when someone files a grievance, we follow up on it immediately, not just to hold residents accountable to community rules, but to find out what's really going on beneath the surface. Because one thing is for sure—it's never about the dishes.

> BREACHES IN CONDUCT TYPICALLY HAPPEN JUST BEFORE SOMEONE RELAPSES, SO WHEN SOMEONE FILES A GRIEVANCE, WE FOLLOW UP ON IT IMMEDIATELY.

If we want to help people uncover the truth about who they really are, we must first discover the truth about who Jesus really is. As you might have guessed, this is a trial-and-error progression that requires grace, patience, and a healthy dose of humility for all involved. Unfortunately, many Christian recovery circles struggle to harness these attributes when people relapse—falling back into addiction, mental health problems, or suicidal thoughts after a period of freedom. If we're honest, we'll admit the truth: relapse is an embarrassing inconvenience to us. We struggle to see the reasons why a person's "failure" matters when we have put our programs (and even ourselves) at the center of their stories. We care more about seeing people sober than we do about seeing them whole. And I believe we are collectively called to more than that.

WHAT HAPPENS AFTER THE HEALING?

As Christians, we don't know what to do with relapse any more than we know what to do with sin. We pore over the Gospels, believing in faith to see the perfect one-eighties we choose to infer from miraculous stories of healing and deliverance. But is perpetual perfection really the point God was trying to make when He inspired His Word and put His healing power on display through Jesus? What happens *after* the healing?

Sometimes I wonder what the paralytic man did later in the day after Jesus told him, *"Get up, take your mat and walk"* (Mark 2:9). Or the two blind men Jesus healed just after Jairus's daughter "woke up" in Matthew 9—what did they do next? What did Jesus's friend Lazarus do after Jesus raised him from the dead in John 11? We assume they all lived happily ever after...and maybe they did.

But what if that's not the case? Maybe the former paralytic walked home, rolled out his mat, and laid down again because it's all he knew how to do. Maybe the blind men put their newfound sight to further use at the local brothel. Maybe the rest of Lazarus's day was great—but even he died again, didn't he? Relapse never dismisses the miracle. But even a miracle doesn't mean relapse isn't a possibility.

> WHEN WE ENCOUNTER MOUNTAINTOP MIRACLE MOMENTS DURING A RECOVERY JOURNEY, OUR HOPE IS THAT WE NEVER GO BACK TO THAT OLD WAY OF LIFE.

When we encounter mountaintop miracle moments during a recovery journey, our hope—for ourselves and for the people we love and lead—is that we never go back to that old way of life. We know it's possible because God's Word says it is. *"Our old self was crucified with him so that the body ruled by sin might be done away with"* (Romans 6:6). The "old man" sinner is dead and gone; we are now fierce, full-of-fire saints, children of a loving Father God! The problem is, even when we know this, we may not actually believe it or receive it. And even when we do, we can be quick to forget when the stresses of life come back in full force.

This rang especially true for a former member of our Timothy Initiative community—let's call him "Bo."

Bo's struggles went beyond his addiction. He was on disability for a partial paralysis in his right leg and walked with a cane. Because his disability made it difficult to pull his weight on our work crews, he struggled to bond with the other men. A promised-land lifestyle was in plain view for Bo. But like the tribes of Reuben and Gad, who petitioned to Moses to settle on the far side of the Jordan River instead of going into the promised land (see Numbers 32:1–5), Bo wasn't sure he could handle life on the other side with his physical limitations.

When I talked to Bo about the issue, he found the courage to express this concern to our leadership team. We responded by doing what any loving church family would do—we prayed for him! Our T.I. crew laid hands on Bo one night and prayed simple, earnest prayers for healing of his leg in Jesus's name. I'll never forget the raptured look on Bo's face as he stood up straight, held his leg in the air, and bent it at the knee again and again—for the first time in nine years! Bo took off running through the streets, praising God, and waving his cane wildly in the air above him as he went. The Holy Spirit's healing handprint remained red hot on his fair-skinned leg for days afterward.

Bo had reached the mountaintop summit. His disability was healed, he was high on Jesus, and for the first time, he knew his identity as a child of God was secure. Until he forgot. Less than a week after his healing, Bo relapsed. And in retrospect, we should have seen it coming. One Sunday afternoon, he took $350 worth of food stamps to sell for drugs, stole a prominent donor family's car from our property, and spent three days holed up in a motel, drowning himself in drugs and prostitutes. Concerned for his well-being and wondering how on earth I would explain the incident to our donor—who we were supposed to pick up from the airport on Thursday in their vehicle—I was already wide awake when my phone rang early Thursday morning. It was Bo. Standing broken on my front porch with the donor's vehicle parked awkwardly in the driveway behind him, he asked unassumingly if he could still come home.

Many programs would consider Bo a fail-out statistic because of his relapse and create concrete barriers to reentry. Since Bo was not part of a program but part of our Timothy Initiative family, we welcomed him back, restored him gently, and immediately plugged him back into all aspects of community life.

The following Sunday, our simple church was standing-room only. Among the thirty-some attendees squeezed into my tiny living room were special guests Kevin and Kathleen—the same prominent donors whose car Bo had just stolen. We had picked Kathleen up from the airport Thursday as promised, but I had yet to meet with the couple in private to explain to them what had happened with Bo and their car. She didn't seem to notice anything different about the vehicle—or if she did, she didn't let on.

Thick as the air seemed, the meeting went on in its usual way. Bo maintained a quiet but fidgety nervousness during a more-than-timely teaching on forgiveness. *In order to extend grace, we need to know what it is we are really forgiving...* Bo couldn't hold it in any longer. He jumped to his feet mid-teaching, tripped over a few worshippers sitting on the floor, and stood petrified in front of our esteemed donors.

"Kevin, Kathleen, I'm so sorry," Bo choked through tears. "I'm so sorry I stole your car. I'm so sorry I smoked crack in it and had sex with a prostitute in the backseat. I'm so sorry..."

Time stood still as we all stared—hearts racing, mouths gaping. A three-days-sober resident was ugly crying in front of one of our biggest donors, admitting he had stolen his car and committed unspeakable acts inside it! Kevin and Kathleen exchanged wide-eyed glances. They looked at me, then back at Bo, who was still sobbing. After what seemed like an eternity, Kevin spoke.

"Bo," he beamed as he met his offender's eyes. "Don't give it another thought. We forgive you."

> RADICAL FORGIVENESS MAY BE RECKLESS BY THE WORLD'S STANDARDS, BUT IT MIRRORS THE HEART OF A GOOD FATHER GOD WHO NEVER GROWS WEARY OF EXTENDING GRACE TO US.

Just like that. Kevin and Kathleen's immediate response of forgiveness would be considered downright reckless in the eyes of some. No shaming? No ultimatums? No probationary periods to see if he would be allowed to stay in the family? It may have been reckless by the world's standards—but it mirrored the heart of a good Father God who never grows weary of extending grace to us. And for Bo, it made all the difference.

WHO'S TO BLAME?

Even when there is a moment of miraculous healing in a recovery journey like Bo's, we fall short when we expect the recipient to walk out a perfect existence after the mountaintop moment. Truth is, after such a high, just about everything pales in comparison. People like Bo can easily forget who they really are and fall back into old ways of thinking and behaving. There is bound to be a valley following every mountaintop. But without valleys, there would be no mountaintops to reach in the first place.

When people in Christian recovery relapse, leaders typically blame it on a faith issue, a sin issue, or both. While the Uncovery implores us to get to the real reasons why relapse happened, it's even more important not to jump to spiritual conclusions. Yes, there may be a faith issue. Yes, there may be a sin issue. But there may also be a medical issue, a community issue, or an identity issue. When we're tempted to snap to judgment, we must lay aside our cynicism and ask ourselves instead, *What else might be true?* This open-minded, open-hearted approach gut-checks our intentions and positions us for deep and honest conversations with people who relapse. In that condemnation-free environment, they can be free to open up and *uncover* the real reason why they relapsed. And when they find the true cause, they can name it and deal with it, making future relapses less likely.

We, the church, need to adjust our expectations of people in recovery from addiction, mental health problems, and suicidal thoughts and learn how to see relapses for what they really are—a part of the journey. Relapses are extremely likely, especially in the first few years of a person's recovery. While we certainly don't want to dismiss or welcome relapse, we can change the way we respond when it occurs. Instead of resetting our "days sober" counters back to zero and shaming people into false repentance, we can offer individualized, person-centered care. Instead of handing down punitive measures and threats, we can invite them to participate in the Uncovery and find healing in all the right places. Relapse may be an important and even necessary part of their journey—and we need to learn to love them well through it.

THREE KEY QUESTIONS TO ASK

When someone in my community relapses, I ask many questions, but there are three primary ones that get to the heart of the issue.

1. WHY DO YOU THINK YOU RELAPSED?

People don't relapse because they want to. They relapse because they're trying to escape pain, and they might not even know where the pain is coming from. Try not to be discouraged if the initial answer to this question is, "I don't know," because that's often true. Resist the urge to tell them why you think it happened; their relapse is not personal, and it's not about you. Inviting them to retrace their steps before relapse can help frame the real reasons why it happened and identify triggers to be avoided in the future. It can also help them uncover potential underlying causes for their behavior, which can bring breakthrough and healing in their life. Listen objectively, without judgment, and be sure to repeat back what you hear them say so they can confirm you understand. They may not remember everything initially and that's okay. Pray with them and ask the Holy Spirit to help them supernaturally remember key moments.

2. HOW LONG HAS IT BEEN SINCE YOUR LAST RELAPSE?

I don't ask this question to make people turn in their sober token chips, go back to step zero, or feel ashamed. I ask because it's an indicator of progress in someone's recovery journey. If this last stretch of sobriety was longer than the one before it, it shows positive progress. If it was shorter, it's an indication that they may need more intensive support from our community. Relapse can actually help a person can see firsthand whether they're improving or not, and they can set specific and measurable goals of accountability going forward. Since studies show relapse is less likely after longer periods of time, I always explain that the goal isn't to push to the finish but to keep a steady pace to run the race in front of them with strength, dignity, and hope.

3. WHAT'S YOUR NEW BOTTOM LINE?

Going cold turkey rarely works, if ever. While we can't condone self-destructive, abusive, or illegal behaviors, we can have grace for clear and sustainable progress in someone's unique journey. If a person addicted to heroin only drinks alcohol for a week but doesn't shoot up, guess what? That's a win. If a person addicted to sex switches from prostitutes to porn, that's progress. Acknowledge that growth and honor it. Allowing the individual to express the steps they wish to take toward a promised-land life— not just what we want for them—is liberating and empowering. When we tell them, "You'd better get sober and stay sober—or else," they're likely to rebel. But when they come to the conclusion on their own, they're more prone to try again for the right reasons. As they continually establish new bottom lines, they will continue to move toward complete freedom.

> ALLOWING THE INDIVIDUAL TO EXPRESS THE STEPS THEY WISH TO TAKE TOWARD A PROMISED-LAND LIFE IS LIBERATING AND EMPOWERING.

Speaking of lines, it's important to know when to draw them and when to wipe them out. Many people I love and lead through recovery have spent time in jail. They know how to walk the line, both literally and figuratively. You see, correctional institutions often have yellow or white painted lines along corridors, in high-traffic areas, and around exercise yards. While in transit or exercising, inmates are required to walk single file along the line without straying or they'll be punished.

There are sad and sobering parallels to traditional recovery in this example. In our sobriety, we walk the line. In our relationships, we walk the line. In our sanity, we walk the line. We walk the line to avoid punishment, stay under the radar, and earn our way back into grace—until we've had our fill of meaningless, perpetual compliance, until another step on that blasted line to nowhere would be worse than death. And then, we stray. If we really want to tap into Uncovery territory, we must be willing to step outside the lines and draw new, more productive lines of our own.

Here's the real rub. Most recovery programs don't leave any room for relapse, leaving leaders and participants alike at a loss when it happens. Those famous twelve steps can feel pretty darn lockstep legalistic, taking people back to step zero when relapse happens, as if the work they did to date meant nothing. What's more, the perpetual *anonymous* mentality keeps hurting people in hiding. Being seen, heard, and loved are critical for true healing to happen. I believe valuing vulnerability over anonymity is the key, but most of our standard programs work the other way around.

Finally, purely quantitative celebration and reward methods like chips, meetings made, and even on-time sign-ins can actually hurt more than they help. They strongly imply that the expectation is perfection. None of us will ever be perfect.

We need to be prepared and disciplined in the radical way we are called to love. We need to explore qualitative measures along the recovery journey in addition to quantitative ones. How are things going at work? How are relationships with your family? What does the rest of your life look like outside of recovery meetings? If we can't see progress in these areas in addition to base-level sobriety and program participation measures, we will fail to have an accurate view of any program's success.

MUCH-NEEDED REFORM

As Christian recovery leaders, we don't do what we do just to make the world a better place. We're bringing glory to God by sharing who we know Him to be and inviting others to get to know Him better. Each recovery journey is as unique as the person living it, and we must be willing to go beyond basic recovery into *Uncovery* territory. After all, we're not trying to help people get back to the life that led them into addiction, mental health problems, and suicidal thoughts in the first place. Who wants to recover *that* life? Instead, we must be willing to go deeper—to help people discover who they really are and build a promised-land life that's not just a sober life, but a transformed one. This is the heart of the Uncovery.

> WE MUST BE WILLING TO HELP PEOPLE DISCOVER WHO THEY REALLY ARE AND BUILD A TRANSFORMED, PROMISED-LAND LIFE. THIS IS THE HEART OF THE UNCOVERY.

Outside of structured meetings, an even larger problem exists in inpatient rehabilitation programs and insurance-supported counseling. These not only don't allow for relapse, but they also rush the recovery process so much it's a wonder anyone can stay sober. Getting and staying sober takes more than a thirty-day detox, six months of counseling, or even a year of closely monitored rehabilitation. Most rehabilitation programs are not designed around what the recovering individual needs, but what their insurance providers are willing to cover. This is not only a place of much-needed societal reform, but a place where the church must be willing to pick up the baton when clinical support drops off. It's going to take the whole church to accomplish this, not just those of us in recovery ministry leadership. Otherwise, we will see burnout at unprecedented levels.

So how do we, the church, step up to meet this growing need? Checking boxes on Sunday mornings and even Wednesday nights isn't going to cut it. The solution lies not in *doing* church but *being* the church. It will mean breaking outside the walls of our places of worship to be the hands and feet of Jesus wherever we go. It will mean loving radically and inviting people into our lives to build real and lasting relationships. It will mean rebuilding the Acts 2 church in modern times and finding our places in it. Most of all, it will mean level-setting our collective expectations for how we think someone's recovery journey should go—and being willing to extend grace as our beloved relapsed prodigals find their way back home again.

DO WHATEVER IT TAKES

Scientific studies show that true, lasting recovery takes more than thirty days, six months, or even a year. In fact, for many struggling with addiction, mental health problems, and suicidal thoughts, it may take three years or more for the brain's neuropathways to rewire back to some semblance of normalcy, especially in the pleasure-reward centers. For some, this brain healing can happen naturally in the absence of substance abuse or continued trauma, putting the full fingerprint of our divine DNA on display. For others, it can take a customized combination of therapy, medication, counseling, meetings, and other whole-life interventions, proving once again that we were all created for long-term relationship. The bottom line is the brain *can* heal, especially with multi-year abstinence. As we learn to believe for the miracle *and* respect the journey with each individual we're called to love and lead, we will enter into Uncovery territory—loving without limits, especially through relapse. These means no rigid time constraints, no lofty ultimatums, no shame or condemnation, just unconditional love for who they truly are.

When you come alongside someone through their recovery journey, keep a ballpark estimate of three years in mind. Not because it will take that long—or because it will *only* take that long—but because it may take longer, or it may take less time. Jesus once told Peter he needed to forgive his brother not three times as the Torah commanded, nor seven times as Peter so generously suggested, but seventy-seven times or seventy times seven. (See Matthew 18:21–22.) Christ's implication was that we are to forgive *however many times it takes*. We're called to be fellow travelers on a journey toward a promised-land life with people who are struggling—not for thirty days or a year, not for as long as they comply with the rules, or as long as they continue to make quantifiable progress, *but for however long it takes.* Some days, it feels all-consuming, but it's in losing our life for Jesus that we find true life. (See Matthew 16:25.) It's that dying to self that brings the revelation we want to see.

If three years sounds like a long time to have to be there for someone in a recovery capacity, consider this: Jesus walked the earth, fully Man and fully God, for thirty-three years. He only spent about *three* of those years in active ministry. In those three years, He preached truth to thousands, had a city-to-city following of seventy or so, and kept close company with twelve disciples *"whom he also designated apostles"* (Luke 6:13). He gave His whole heart—the same heart required for recovery ministry—to three of those twelve, Peter, James and John, preparing them for more responsibility than the others.

Jesus never hesitated to meet struggling strangers in the moment, but He would more often than not train up and rely on the rest of the church to continue the journey with the individual. The point? No one person can take responsibility for the physical, mental, and emotional health of the entire world. Jesus didn't even try to do this, and you shouldn't either. But you can journey with one, two, or maybe even three people for as long as it takes. You could pour into the lives of twelve and put a life worth emulating on display for seventy. You may never preach to the masses, but your voice and your testimony speaks volumes. If we can take any insight from the life and ministry of Jesus, the Man, it's that a whole lot can happen in three years! The best part is that Jesus promised us we will do even greater things than He did in His three years of ministry because of the power of the Holy Spirit in us.

*I tell you this timeless truth: The person who follows me in faith, believing in me, will do the same mighty miracles that I do—**even greater miracles than these because I go to be***

with my Father! *For I will do whatever you ask me to do when you ask me in my name. And that is how the Son will show what the Father is really like and bring glory to him. Ask me anything in my name, and I will do it for you!*

(John 14:12–14 TPT)

This promise isn't meant to make you think you *should* do even more than Jesus did. But it is an invitation to each and every follower of Jesus to learn how to ask God the Father, "What more would You have me do?" The answer He gives may shock you. Rebuilding the Acts 2 church in modern times and finding our place in it starts with full-on surrender to God. This means making a commitment to do only what the Father is doing and say only what the Father is saying, like Jesus did.

For me, this meant a radical lifestyle change and a call to refine, reform, and enhance recovery programming to include supplemental and ongoing support. For you, this could mean asking God to highlight even one person you're meant to journey with for as long as it takes. It may mean taking a hard look at what's working (and what's not working) in your personal and corporate ministries and being willing to change directions as God leads you. It won't be easy. But it will be worth it.

Whatever you see the Father doing and whatever you hear Him saying, my prayer is that you will watch, listen, and do whatever He asks of you. Whatever it takes. Trust me—you don't want to miss out on a chance to be part of His work.

QUESTIONS FOR REFLECTION

1. What comes to mind when you hear the word "relapse"?

_____

_____

_____

_____

_____

2. In what ways could relapses be seen as opportunities?

_____

_____

_____

_____

3. Does three years sound like a long time to walk with someone through the Uncovery? Why or why not?

_____

_____

_____

_____

5

RETHINKING SOBRIETY

Jesus never said the world would know we're His disciples
by how long it's been since our last relapse.
—Brad McCoy

If recovery is about getting back what's been lost, the Uncovery is about an exchange—trading an old and broken life for a new one, letting go of a false identity, and embracing a better one rooted in truth. It takes some time for people to get from where they are now to where they want to be in recovery. It takes learning and unlearning, practice, and perseverance from both the recovering individuals and the people journeying alongside them. It takes an intentional shift from a fixed mindset to a growth mindset.

A "fixed mindset" assumes people never change. Our intellect, our creativity, our resilience, and even our personalities are believed to be both static and given. Polarizing labels like *smart* or *dumb*, *good* or *bad*, *clean* or *dirty*, and *fast* or *slow* are used to compartmentalize and judge people and processes. The only way people with a fixed mindset can hope to find success is through endless striving toward lofty, set standards. Failure is not an option. This common all-or-nothing mindset is detrimental to healing and personal growth, especially for people in recovery.

A "growth mindset," on the other hand, assumes people can and do change. Failure isn't seen as fatal, but as an opportunity to stretch, grow, and course-correct.

People typically assume a fixed mindset or a growth mindset in early childhood, setting the tone for their behavior, successes, relationships, and overall capacity for happiness and fulfillment. To be fair, traditional recovery methods aren't necessarily growth averse. Twelve-step programs show at least one possible pathway for progress, which is a good thing. However, the labeling and often legalistic success measures that go hand in hand with recovery programming can perpetuate a fixed mindset that sets people up for failure.

> THE LABELING AND OFTEN LEGALISTIC SUCCESS MEASURES THAT GO HAND IN HAND WITH RECOVERY PROGRAMMING CAN PERPETUATE A FIXED MINDSET THAT SETS PEOPLE UP FOR FAILURE.

Case in point: group meeting introductions. When our identities are reinforced by how we present ourselves to others, "Hi, my name is George, and I'm an alcoholic" becomes a fixed trait. When taken too literally, this type of introduction can be a destructive declaration over oneself that reinforces the old, broken life recovering people need to trade for a new one. This type of introduction also teeters on the line of celebrating the struggle rather than one's progress toward victory over it. Even leading with softer language such as, "Hi, I'm George, and I struggle with alcohol" still implies permanence and focuses on the struggle over the individual. We may as well say something like, "Hi, I'm George, and I'll always be an alcoholic." No matter how long people stay sober or how much progress people make on their recovery journey, this language can brand them for life. When we tell struggling people they'll struggle

forever, they'll believe us—and they'll keep on struggling by faith!
Stigmatizing labels breed discrimination, especially in the church,
and it makes people want to hide. And if history has shown us
anything, it's that when we hide, we fall—hard.

No one is immune to the harmful effects of labeling. In the
recovery group meetings I'm privileged to lead and participate in,
I'm much more interested in helping people adopt language that
affirms who they really are—beloved children of a good Father
God on a journey toward a promised-land life. We don't attach
our struggles to our names during meeting introductions. I care
less about what brought them to the meeting and more about celebrating their choice to come at all. For some of our newer residents, this shift in language is difficult; false identities can be hard
to shake, especially when they've been reinforced in other recovery
circles for so long. But in time, with an affirmed identity intact,
people can name and deal with their struggles free of shame in a
healthy, discipling environment.

Christian recovery group meetings usually look and feel more
like corporate worship than active discipleship. Group rules, timed
responses, and perpetual anonymity help to keep the meeting
on-time and on-topic, but they don't always foster authentic relationships. Recovery takes true discipleship—and true discipleship
can't happen corporately. It takes a calibration of invitation and
challenge that requires both permission and intimacy, and this
is difficult if not impossible to systemize or schedule. Instead of
asking how you can run more efficient and effective meetings, ask
God what more He would have you do to love and support your
people once the meetings are over.

Labels aside, tracking hours, days, weeks, months, and even
years sober doesn't always respect the fullness of someone's recovery journey. Yes, it's important to celebrate sobriety milestones.
But it's also important to remember that a sober person may not
be living a transformed life. What's more, when people get sober

in one area, new struggles often rise to the surface that previously weren't obvious. Just as behavioral outbursts are *never really about the dishes*, the underlying causes around addiction can uncover mental health problems people never knew they had. People who struggle with addictions and compulsive behaviors often trade one for another, making true sobriety or even abstinence incredibly difficult to quantify and track. The answer to the question, "Are you sober?" becomes "Sober from what?" And when a person can't determine whether they're really sober or not, chips and other rewards become meaningless—and in some cases, even harmful.

THE UNDERLYING CAUSES AROUND ADDICTION CAN UNCOVER MENTAL HEALTH PROBLEMS PEOPLE NEVER KNEW THEY HAD.

When my co-author Brit received her one-year chip in front of the masses one evening at a prominent recovery program's leadership summit, she didn't have the heart to tell them she hadn't exactly been "sober" from her eating disorder for the whole year. Yes, she had attended meetings regularly for a year and made significant progress. Yes, she had learned the truth about her identity and helped others learn it, too. Yes, she'd had weeks and even months-long stints of sobriety that helped her identify common triggers as she healed her body, mind, and soul. But even in those small victories, she hadn't exactly volunteered the many, many times she'd relapsed back into bulimic behavior that year—as recently as a month before that night. She returned to her seat, flipped the blue plastic between her fingers, and swallowed hard. She tried to mentally dismiss the countless *other* ways traditional recovery purists wouldn't consider her "sober" yet—her codependency, her anger, her fear…oh, and her occasional half a bottle of wine to chase the day away. She sure looked sober on the surface, but the chip actually reinforced her false narrative as well as her need to hide in plain sight.

Here's the hard truth: When we value days sober over brave daily choices to build a promised-land life, people continue to relapse, unable to achieve such unreasonably perfectionistic, all-or-nothing standards. But when we choose to love uncondition-ally, celebrate the small victories, learn from our failures, and con-tinually affirm a true, God-given identity in people, we see lives transformed.

BUILD THE PLANE WHILE YOU FLY IT

If hurt people *hurt people*, helped people *help people*. Most recovery program leaders come by their positions honestly, not out of obligation or with an agenda. Recovery leaders are just people like you and me. Usually, they've struggled with addiction, mental health problems, and/or suicidal thoughts themselves, but they've discovered at least some tangible level of freedom. They want to help others taste the freedom they've found. That's beautiful.

But the problem is, even as fellow travelers on a journey, our paths to transformation are unique. Each and every roadblock is a critical part of what will one day be a living testimony. The Uncovery takes recovery leaders beyond the role of "helper" to identity-driven liberator. Free people *free people* when they do it in Jesus's name.

One of the most beautiful things about Christian recovery is the way struggling people are invited into leadership roles when they would be otherwise overlooked. Even in twelve-step program-ming, new attendees are given a job and invited into the fullness of community life early on. This means people still in the throes of struggle can be invited to read Scripture, lead worship, facilitate small groups, and more.

While most leaders exercise caution and discernment with the volume and types of leadership roles newly recovering individuals are invited to assume, the stigma of "being ready" to take on these roles in recovery is almost nonexistent. God doesn't call the qualified—He commissions the willing and qualifies them along the way. Leadership isn't something you fight to earn but something you grow into. To people in recovery who are invited into this build-the-plane-while-you-fly-it style of leadership, it's called *grace*—unmerited favor that reflects the heart of the Father.

Grace is a controversial topic in Christian recovery. Let's be honest—it's a controversial topic in the whole church! There are about as many interpretations of how God chooses to extend grace as there are people in need of it. Based on biblical truth and the life of Jesus, I am convinced that God initiates grace that moves people to repentance, not the other way around. This keeps my mission clear. If I can help broken people know how loved and forgiven they already are, it's much easier for them to receive the Father's grace by faith and step into their life's true calling.

> IF I CAN HELP BROKEN PEOPLE KNOW HOW LOVED AND FORGIVEN THEY ALREADY ARE, IT'S MUCH EASIER FOR THEM TO RECEIVE THE FATHER'S GRACE BY FAITH AND STEP INTO THEIR LIFE'S TRUE CALLING.

From a practical standpoint, this can be a challenge. It's one I learned the hard way. When we first launched the Timothy Initiative, we had no rules. None! We were so frustrated with the legalistic nature of traditional recovery, we went full-speed in the other direction. It took us all of twenty-five minutes to realize that our zero-rules approach wasn't going to work. Thankfully, there was grace to cover our grace giving. Our commitment to breaking the mold allowed us to start fresh, implementing community guidelines that encouraged transformation instead of fear-based, walk-the-line rules that demand perfection. We didn't look to other recovery programs for standardized rules. We determined which guidelines were necessary for a sober living community. More importantly, we determined which ones we could toss out in order to keep people on a path toward transformation.

HELPING A "RECOVERY PRO"

This fluid assessment became especially important to me when I met Joe Carr, who "failed out" of traditional recovery without even relapsing.

Joe had been in a prominent Christian recovery rehab for six months. He was as clean as a whistle. It was Joe's second time through this particular rehab, so in his mind, he already knew the boxes to check, the words to say, and the rules to follow to graduate. Joe grew up in a legalistic church environment, so it was easy for him to go through the motions. But when he was asked to hold a smartphone for a ministry leader, he was caught checking one of his social media accounts. He immediately received a "black tag," the highest level of lockdown restriction.

Less than twenty-four hours later, Joe was on the front steps of the rehab facility with nothing to his name but ten dollars and a duffel bag of belongings. With only two weeks until his graduation, Joe had been *kicked out* of the program for a minor infraction—without even breaking his sobriety. His anxious thoughts pulled him toward spending that ten bucks on getting high... but instead of calling his dealer, he called a friend, who offered to introduce Joe to me.

To our surprise, Joe arrived at my office with his mom. She gave him a ride but refused to take him in again—for good reason. After years of being exploited financially and emotionally by Joe, she knew she wasn't going to be able to walk with her son on this leg of his recovery journey. I could tell in my first few minutes with Joe that he was a recovery pro. He certainly knew how to work a program! But despite being sober, he was still in deep denial about his struggles and about as far away from God as a person could be.

Joe failed at traditional recovery, but I believe traditional recovery failed him—and he needed something really different. Joe found the transition into nontraditional recovery confusing. He discovered the Timothy Initiative had very few *rules*, an unusual amount of trust, and a sober-living community that looked less like rehab and more like a big family.

Suspicious, Joe kept his guard up and tried to figure out how to work the system. And when he learned there was no system to work, he began to challenge everything—especially in Bible studies. The Word of God was such sandpaper on his soul that he struggled to even say the name "Jesus" without feeling like a complete hypocrite. Joe became combative and arrogant with a default "no" response to any request. But in time, the same good Father God he struggled to see was put on full display by our community. For the first time in Joe's life, the gospel was made tangible by people who were willing to go beyond twelve steps and be Jesus to him. After a dark season of transition, he simply couldn't deny God's love any longer. Joe rededicated his life to Jesus and was baptized on my back deck.

A few months after his rededication, I felt led to ask Joe to step into a deeper level of leadership with the Timothy Initiative. It was a huge risk, which is how I knew it was from God and not from me. I asked Joe to head the construction teams for Initiative Builds, the revenue-generating work teams for the Timothy Initiative—not as an employee, but as owner of the company. This big ask resulted in months of repeated "no's" from Joe, who despite his construction background felt unqualified to take on such a huge responsibility for the ministry. In time, Joe's emphatic "no" became a humble "yes," and I gifted him the business. Now six years later, Joe has created a thriving business model that provides work opportunities for our residents and a sustainable income stream for the ministry. Joe and his wife Lindsay still live in our community as some of T.I.'s most trusted leaders and friends.

Some struggle with the idea of inviting people into recovery leadership before they're ready. Putting important tasks into the hands of people they perceive as unstable seems way too risky—even reckless. However, I'm convinced that these barriers in the church and in other facets of society are why so many powerful leaders struggle in silence and then fall—hard. When perfection is the only possible standard, even our best, brightest, and most balanced don't have a prayer.

> WHEN PERFECTION IS THE ONLY POSSIBLE STANDARD, EVEN OUR BEST, BRIGHTEST, AND MOST BALANCED DON'T HAVE A PRAYER.

When the manuscript for this book was being developed in 2020, I watched in horror as faith leader after faith leader seemed to fall from grace, crushed under the pressure of what the world calls "a year from hell." Headlines of scandal, addiction, suicide, racism, sexism, fascism, and abuse wreaked havoc on the Christian community with each bold and condemning word. In response, most of the church seemed to either polarize or paralyze. As far too many of us grabbed torches and pitchforks or fell painfully silent, we realized another potential pitfall to traditional recovery. Authority void of true identity is a recipe for disaster because when people have power, it is so much easier to hide.

THE PROBLEM WITH POWER

Being in a position of authority has both emotional and biological implications. Research shows it even has a drug-like effect on the brain.[14] Power, or even the perception of power, provides a dopamine hit that simulates an addictive high. The result can be both good and bad. In moderate amounts, that dopamine hit can enhance cognitive function, unearthing new levels of creativity and resilience that are critical to leadership, progress, and even survival. But dopamine spikes and withdrawals can cause poor judgment, self-absorption, and obsession, making leaders feel like they're invincible and accountable to no one. This is when we see leaders fall. They're forced to put up a fake, plastic façade so they can continue to look the part of a leader, while oftentimes struggling with the very problems they preach against. With no one to actively disciple them and hold them accountable, they're free to live a compartmentalized double life if they choose. They may even be able to convince their subordinates and followers to help them cover up their messes when they're eventually—and inevitably—exposed.

Leadership is a necessary call in recovery, in the church, and in every part of life. But absolute, unchecked power isn't healthy anywhere, especially in the recovery space. Few leaders step up only to seek corruption. I believe this in my heart, and I want to honor the true intentions of even those leaders who have publicly fallen from grace. Recovery is for everyone—especially for the people we assume would never need it. Faithful checks and balances can be helpful, but it's more crucial that we build authentic communities where vulnerability is valued over plastic perfection. Leaders who are free to admit their own struggles can secure the love and accountability they need. What's more, they can also inspire subordinates and followers to name and deal with their own struggles, too. The most transformational leaders are the ones who consider themselves fellow travelers on a journey with the ones they love and lead. They're last in line, not first. (See Matthew 20:16.) They're building empires not on the backs of their people but on a solid foundation of truth.

---

14. Nayef Al-Rodhan, "The neurochemistry of power has implications for political change," *The Conversation*, February 28, 2014, theconversation.com/the-neurochemistry-of-power-has-implications-for-political-change-23844.

But here's the thing: Leaders can only step into authentic vulnerability when the community will not only tolerate it but encourage and reward it. Instead of putting them on a pedestal, we need to invite leaders at all levels into the same safe places and warm embraces we offer to the least of these.

> WHEN WE CALL PEOPLE INTO POSITIONS OF LEADERSHIP BECAUSE OF THE PUBLIC, VISIBLE MILESTONES THEY'VE ATTAINED, WE CAN ACTUALLY SET THEM UP FOR FAILURE.

Appointing leaders in the recovery space takes discernment and surrender. There's no one-size-fits-all model or surefire set of regulations that will cover it. I'm convinced there is no career path that will work every time—and here's why. When we call people into positions of leadership because of the public, visible milestones they've attained—a one-year chip, a new job landed, a family restored—we can actually set them up for failure. As soon as we say, "They're not struggling anymore, so they're ready to lead," we throw the door wide open for relapse and abuse of power. On the other hand, having unrealistic leadership expectations of people still actively struggling with addiction, mental health problems, and suicidal thoughts can be just as damaging.

In the Bible, James says it plainly: *"Not many of you should become teachers, my fellow believers, because you know that we who teach will be judged more strictly"* (James 3:1). And Paul brings it home in his first letter to Timothy: *"Never be in a hurry about appointing a church leader. Do not share in the sins of others. Keep yourself pure"* (1 Timothy 5:22 NLT).

It's my personal belief that leadership in the Christian recovery space cannot be merit-based. We can never fully know how someone is doing on their recovery journey beyond what they share and what we see. Increasing responsibilities or acknowledging authority on this basis alone is foolishness.

GOD CALLED MISFITS

God is famous for calling and equipping the most unqualified misfits to be the ones to bring His kingdom here on the earth. Blue-collar fishermen, tax collectors, prostitutes, murderers— *these* were the people Jesus called to follow Him into leadership. He wasn't being edgy, ironic, or even inclusive. He was being sensitive to the divine DNA present in each of these would-be saints and inviting them to follow Him and lead others because the Father told Him to do so. Jesus knew that people who had been forgiven much would love all the more—and many of the ones He called were willing to die for the sake of the gospel.

Did these appointed leaders walk out their callings perfectly, free of corruption? Of course not! Judas Iscariot hid in plain sight and fell—hard. Yet even in his betrayal, he helped to fulfill God's purposes. Peter—the rock upon whom Jesus built His church (see Matthew 16:18)— faltered again and again and again. And he was restored by Jesus just as many times. Years later, even the apostle Paul still struggled with some of the same sins he preached against. (See Romans 7:15–25.) But God taught him humility and vulnerability in his teaching so he could identify with people who struggle. In and through the struggles and failures of these leaders, they were part of a motley crew who made the name of Jesus known around the world.

INTANGIBLE TRANSFORMATION

The promised-land life we want to help people build comes not by way of baseline sobriety, but multidimensional transformation. But most recovery programs still focus on days, weeks, months, and years sober because personal transformation is extremely difficult to measure through hard data and numbers. If sobriety is our only measure of success, it means people have to start all over again with every bump in the road. This causes burnout and fails to honor the work that's been done. The ramifications of imperfection cause more and more people to hide in plain sight. Anonymity perpetuates shame, which perpetuates hiding, which perpetuates addiction, mental health problems, and suicidal thoughts. When people know they're being judged, they believe they must carry the burden of their struggles alone—*in many cases, to the point of death*—even after Jesus died on the cross to redeem those same struggles.

We need to find ways to qualify success in recovery measures beyond quantifiable means. The *Journal of the American Medical Association* reports that 40 to 60 percent of people in recovery will relapse at least once within the first year.[15] Keep in mind, those numbers are based on the historical number of people who *reported* that they relapsed, so the actual figures are probably higher. If more than half of people who get sober will likely have to try again at some point, why do we continue to measure success on quantifiable sobriety data alone? By these measures, recovery doesn't really work—so why even try? What's more, people typically have *multiple* struggles,[16] blurring the lines of quantifiable sobriety as a variety of issues come to the surface during the Uncovery.

> MINISTRY FUNDING IS ALL TOO OFTEN WITHHELD WHEN RECOVERY LEADERS ARE UNABLE TO QUALIFY THE INTANGIBLE ELEMENTS OF RECOVERY.

Now, numbers and data are important evidence markers—I'm not arguing that we should throw them out altogether. But people are not numbers. Lives and souls are at stake. And yet ministry funding is all too often withheld when recovery leaders are unable to qualify the intangible elements of recovery.

15. Jaclyn Schuon, "Why Relapse is Part of Recovery from Drug Abuse and Addiction," April 1, 2020, rehabs.com/is-relapse-normal.
16. "Alcohol and Drug Abuse Statistics," American Addiction Centers, March 11, 2022, americanaddictioncenters.org/rehab-guide/addiction-statistics.

The numbers associated with the Timothy Initiative and the Sober Truth Project most certainly disqualify us from most federal funding opportunities. In no way am I ashamed about this because I know that we're tracking more than baseline sobriety. We knew early on that we were interested in monitoring the intangible elements of recovery, so we chose to operate as an independent entity. We receive no government funding whatsoever. I know this isn't possible for some programs, but I firmly believe the success markers that have come out of our grand experiment will benefit any recovery group, whether secular or Spirit-led, federally funded or grassroots grown. I'm proud to be an independent outlier who might help to better inform the masses.

QUESTIONS TO ASK TO QUALIFY THE INTANGIBLES

Traditional Recovery	The Uncovery
How long have you been sober?	Are you making progress in your journey?
Will you commit to a thirty-day program?	Will you stay as long as you need help?
Are you attending your meetings?	Are you connecting with the community?
When was your last relapse?	Are you going longer between relapses?
Are you following the rules?	Have you had any encounters with God?
Are you meeting curfew?	How are you using your free time?
Have you accepted your struggle?	Have you discovered your true identity?
Can you reenter society?	Are you building a promised-land life?

In my experience, stigmatization beyond addiction, mental health, and suicidal thoughts exists in recovery fundraising. Race, gender, socioeconomic status, sexual orientation, political, and even denominational affiliations can keep the proverbial purse strings tightly closed—and not for the reasons you may think.

For example, many generous philanthropists are slow to give to the Timothy Initiative because that particular ministry is only focused on helping broken men. When a widow or an orphan is in distress, the funds come flooding, but when a man falls into addiction, people assume he deserves it.

Religion that God our Father accepts as pure and faultless is this: to look after orphans and widows in their distress and to keep oneself from being polluted by the world. (James 1:27)

There's no denying these powerful words make it clear that we, the church, are called to advocate for the marginalized, oppressed, and victimized. Jesus said, *"Truly I tell you, whatever you did for one of the least of these brothers and sisters of mine, you did for me"* (Matthew 25:40). But what if *"the least of these"* isn't always obvious?

TRANSFORMING ALL BROKEN PEOPLE

What's more, what if we're called to help broken people transform—regardless of whether the rest of the world might choose to see them as victim or victimizer, captive or prisoner?

Captives are oppressed people, held in bondage against their will. They may do nothing to contribute to the trauma that enslaves them. Prisoners are a different story. In a devastating mix of circumstances and poor choices made, sin and unlawfulness put them where they are. They may have made a choice to enter in, but they can't always make a choice to break free. As leaders, we typically address the problem based on its origin. In a traditional program, the perception is that the individual *chose* addiction, and they're forced to endure a shame-driven recovery process that continually reminds them that it's their own fault that they're in the program.

Most healthy people can identify with both captive and prisoner at some level. But regardless of how we end up in bondage to our struggles, our help comes from the same God. Jesus quoted Isaiah's related prophecy about Himself to the astonishment of listeners at a Nazareth synagogue, calling His people to love and lead like He did:

> *The Spirit of the Lord is on me, because he has anointed me to proclaim good news to the poor. He has sent me to proclaim freedom for the prisoners and recovery of sight for the blind, to set the oppressed free, to proclaim the year of the Lord's favor.* (Luke 4:18–19; also see Isaiah 61:1–2)

> *If the Son sets you free, you will be free indeed.* (John 8:36)

Freedom is not just reserved for the captive, but for the prisoner, too. Although I believe understanding the root causes of our addictions, mental health problems, and suicidal thoughts is critical to the Uncovery, using the root cause as a weapon is not productive or redemptive. We must be willing to go beyond genetic predisposition and generational curses to explore more trauma-informed ministry tactics. This will bring about not only deliverance from bondage but a promised-land life of transformation—even for the ones we don't think deserve it. *Especially* for them. This is the grace we, the church, are called to show, the unmerited favor of a loving Father for everyone.

EMBRACING THE UNCOVERY

Helping people go deeper into their recovery journey—into true Uncovery territory—will require us to affirm and celebrate the moments that go beyond metrics. It's not sobriety that matters but what sobriety can mean for a person's life:

+ Choosing to stay in a marriage that could have ended

+ Nailing a job interview, even if it's not a dream job

+ Getting a clear diagnosis and exploring appropriate therapies and medication

+ Sharing vulnerably about a struggle instead of trying to hide it

+ Finding friends who care enough to convince the person that life is worth living

+ Meeting God as a loving Father through the saving grace of Jesus

These pivotal moments can make all the difference in someone's recovery journey, and we need to make space for them to be acknowledged and celebrated. But more than this, those of us who lead in Christian recovery need to focus on the identity-driven truth and grace that will not only matter in this life, but in the next one.

Years ago, we had a T.I. brother named Randy who became the poster child success story for us in the early days. He came to us from jail with a history of heroin use and defiance to all authority. He had lost everything to his addiction, including his family and his daughter. He couldn't read, had no marketable skills or experience, and had no faith or hope to cling to. In a matter of *months*, the Father rescued Randy's heart, reunited him with his daughter, and positioned him in a community of people who poured into him personally, professionally, and spiritually. He learned to read, stepped up to lead, and loved testifying to God's goodness in his life. Our donors loved this story and would point to Randy as proof positive that the Uncovery works. Our men embraced Randy as a brother and looked to him as a shining example and a beacon of hope.

That sweet season of certainty lasted about six months until the bitter Monday morning when I had to stand before the men and a handful of donors and deliver the news. Randy had relapsed... and was dead. Kevin, the donor who extended reckless grace to our rowdy brother Bo, mentioned in chapter four, took Randy's death especially hard. While processing his grief, he confronted me with tough questions. "Why even bother? Why are we doing this if the end result is just going to be death? All that work, all those resources, all that breakthrough—wasted!"

In that moment, the Lord gave me an answer that still keeps me going through the good and the bad. "We don't do this to get people sober. We do this so people can have a transformative encounter with the Father that lasts for eternity. Life is short— sometimes too short—but death is not the end result for Randy anymore." I believe Randy remains one of the Father's most powerful kingdom success stories.

The Uncovery isn't a program, so there is no new model for others to follow. The Uncovery is a shift in mindset, not method. My hope is that this will be very freeing for leaders of traditional recovery programs because it means there's no need to scrap everything and start over. You know your calling and you know what your community needs. The Uncovery invites you to embrace what's working, let go of what's not, and be open to new ideas and solutions that could make all the difference to the ones you love and lead.

STEPPING INTO UNCOVERY TERRITORY

Here are a handful of suggestions to consider as you step into Uncovery territory.

QUALIFY AS YOU QUANTIFY

As you crunch the numbers for your own records to appease your donors or invite new funding opportunities, consider sharing qualitative information in addition to hard data. Document what can be observed and recorded from your community, even if it can't be counted. Track themes, ideas, and other phenomena, even if there aren't hard-and-fast numbers to go with them. Research shows that although numbers can be used to reinforce our judgments, donors ultimately make decisions based on how the information you share makes them feel.[17] Keep a careful balance of functional and emotional measures in your dashboard of success metrics. Value choices over chips, and you'll win every time.

KNOW AND BE KNOWN

Anonymity can help to create a safe place, especially for those in the early stages of their recovery journey. While honoring anonymity and keeping confidence is key, encouraging long-term secrecy breeds shame. Many of us don't really want to know the fullness of people's messes because they might catch a glimpse of our own. So we get to know a little about someone without really knowing them at all. Struggling as an *unknown* may get people sober for a while, but it won't foster the community they need to transform their lives. Encouraging vulnerability over anonymity—and actually walking it out—helps people feel seen, heard, and loved. And in the act of truly knowing, we can open our hearts and minds to the beauty of being truly known ourselves.

TASTE THE FRUIT OF GROWTH

When we remove perfectionistic, works-based rules and regulations, we create space for progressive transformation. Deliverance

---

17. Elizabeth Pun, "3 Psychological Triggers That Can Help You Win Donations," *Classy* blog, January 7, 2016, www.classy.org/blog/3-psychological-triggers-to-win-donations.

leads to freedom, which makes room for sustainable yet nonlinear transformation. This is the solid ground needed to cultivate a promised-land life that bears the fruits of the Spirit in recovery. Love, joy, peace, patience, kindness, goodness, faithfulness, gentleness, and self-control (see Galatians 5:22–23) are *byproducts* of recovery—not prerequisites! Adopting a growth mindset helps people in recovery *"taste and see that the* LORD *is good"* (Psalm 34:8), even when they're not sure how to peel the proverbial pomegranate yet.

WHAT'S NEXT? ASK GOD

What's next for you, your ministry, or your own recovery journey isn't up to you—it's up to God. So ask Him now, even in this moment, "Father, what more would You have me do?" Acknowledge where your life or ministry has become unmanageable and invite Him to reveal something new for you or your recovery community, something you would never come up with on your own. God's strength is made perfect in our weakness. (See 2 Corinthians 12:9.) And we, the church, need to remember what surrender really looks like: the loving embrace of grace.

QUESTIONS FOR REFLECTION

1. Are you currently in a fixed mindset or a growth mindset?

_____

_____

_____

_____

_____

2. What labels do you use that you need to release?

_____

_____

_____

_____

_____

3. What qualitative, quantitative, tangible, and intangible metrics do you need to track?

_____

_____

_____

_____

_____

6

HEALING VS. CURING

On hearing this, Jesus said to them,
"It is not the healthy who need a doctor, but the sick.
I have not come to call the righteous, but sinners."
—Mark 2:17

"The best way out is always through."

When renowned poet Robert Frost penned these famous words in his 1914 masterpiece "A Servant to Servants," he probably didn't realize the prophetic nature they carried. Through the poetic voice of an overworked, overwhelmed, and unappreciated housewife, Frost speaks plainly to the very real human struggles of loneliness, exhaustion, trauma, and mental illness. In a highly conversational, pithy tone, the woman pours her heart out to a complete stranger, thrilled to have someone—*anyone*—who would listen. And in that brief opportunity to process out loud, she comes to her own conclusion: "The best way out is always through." Not around, not over, not underneath—through.

Some scholars see the woman in Frost's poem as fatalistic, but perhaps Frost's point was that initial deliverance is not the same as transformation. Attempting to bypass God's deliverance is like an expectant mother who is looking for a way to meet her child without going through the pain of labor. Trying to go around painful situations instead of through them can make people miss out on true healing and the beauty of divine growth. When you're going through hell on earth in your recovery journey, sometimes the best and only option is to keep on going.

> SOMETIMES, THE ONLY WAY TO DISCOVER THE TRUTH ABOUT OUR IDENTITY IS BY GOING THROUGH THE REFINING FIRE THAT FINALLY DESTROYS THE LIE.

The journey toward uncovering the truth about our identity is one that's worth taking. And sometimes, the only way to discover that truth is by going through the refining fire that finally destroys the lie. To help people build a promised-land life worth staying sober for, we will all have to get comfortable with life in the wilderness. It's in those painful places of wandering and wondering through the Uncovery that God meets us where we are—to heal our wounds, cure our diseases, and transform our hearts and lives.

HEALING, CURING, AND TRANSFORMATION

The recovery space is broad and wide, spanning both sacred and secular organizations with wildly varying methodologies. This diversity of thought brings so many questions to the table— questions for which we may *think* we already know the answers but are worthy of deeper exploration. Here are three of the most polarizing questions keeping the church and the scientific community at odds with one another. Walk through each of them with an open heart and an open mind, and you might be surprised what God chooses to reveal to you.

1. ARE ADDICTION, MENTAL HEALTH PROBLEMS, AND SUICIDAL THOUGHTS SIN OR SICKNESS?

In the recovery space, there are generally two camps. The first camp, which often operates within the walls of the traditional church, believes addiction, mental health problems, and suicidal thoughts are a result of people's sin and poor choices. The second camp, which often operates within the secular medical community, believes these same struggles are purely physiological issues caused by genetics, trauma, and environment. Admittedly, these are broad generalizations, but they help to explain the black hat/white hat battle that has existed between the spiritual and scientific communities for hundreds if not thousands of years. Sacred groups see medical intervention and therapy as a lack of faith; scientific communities see refusal of therapy and treatment as a lack of wisdom.

EVEN WHEN PEOPLE DO NOTHING TO CONTRIBUTE TO THE TRAUMA THAT LED THEM DOWN A PATH OF DESTRUCTION, AT SOME POINT, MOST PEOPLE BECOME WILLING PARTICIPANTS IN THE AFTERMATH.

So which is it? Are our struggles sin issues or physiological issues? I'd like to suggest that it's not either/or—it's both and then some. Even when people do nothing to contribute to the trauma that led them down a path of destruction, at some point, most people become willing participants in the aftermath. Even when we come from third, fourth, and fifth generation addicted families, we know from Scripture that neither our sin nor our ancestors' sin automatically results in a generational curse. The divine nature attached to our struggles only makes sense through the lens of a good Father God, who would never allow suffering that did not in some way display His power, goodness, and grace. (See John 9:2–3.) However people came to find themselves in bondage, our responsibility is to love and walk alongside sin-sick souls.

2. ARE PEOPLE IN RECOVERY BEING HEALED OR CURED?

Being *cured* is language traditionally attached to professional medical circles, meaning complete elimination of an illness or disease. Being *healed*, on the other hand, describes something that can happen both naturally *and* supernaturally, even when no physical cure is possible. While many see addiction, mental health problems, and suicidal thoughts as defining and even permanent illnesses that require lifelong treatment, others see them as struggles that can be overcome, either by sheer will or by the power of the Holy Spirit.

So which is it? Are we trying to heal addiction, mental health problems, and suicidal thoughts or cure them? I'd like to suggest that it's both. Our struggles can be a direct result of genetic predispositions, trauma, abuse, and, yes, even our own poor and sinful choices. Some struggles will require therapies and medical intervention. Some will require fervent prayer and a whole lot of faith. Most will require both. Whether you are curing a disease or healing a literal or figurative wound, I believe medical professionals and ministry leaders alike can do more of what they do best by leaning on one another for a more holistic, comprehensive, and collaborative approach to recovery.

3. IS IT REALLY OKAY TO HAVE JESUS AND A THERAPIST, TOO?

A much-needed recalibration is taking place regarding mental health, thanks to a widespread secular push to embrace vulnerability and destigmatize therapy and medical intervention for people struggling with addiction, mental health problems, and suicidal thoughts. Admittedly, we, the church, are late to the game on this critical shift. Secular humanists stand with open arms to hurting souls while much of the church remains guarded and in some cases gated, more of a country club for saints than a hospital for sinners. Our reluctance has created extreme dissonance as ministry leaders and laypeople alike scramble to figure out what it means for us to *"walk in the light, as* [Jesus] *is in the light"* (1 John 1:7) while also allowing God to work in and through medical and mental health professionals who may not exactly see Him as a good Father—if they see Him at all. With depression, moral failure, and addiction running rampant through every rank of Christendom, I think it's high time for us to embrace the truth.

Yes, it's okay to have Jesus and a therapist, too.

Hard stop.

LifeWay Research reports that 79 percent of Christians who struggle with mental health problems insist that psychotherapy has been helpful. That number increases to 81 percent for those involved in regular Christian community. What's more, 85 percent of those same individuals insist medication has been helpful, too, and this figure jumps to 90 percent for those involved in regular Christian community.[18] If research shows that therapy and medication can help to improve a Christian's recovery journey, why on earth would we, the church, deprive them of it?

God created humans for relationship. He knew we would need one another to bear our burdens together because the fallen word we live in is just too heavy for any one person to carry alone. If that other person happens to carry knowledge and wisdom that could help to uncover underlying psychological and physiological issues that a twelve-step program or prayer group might not be able to find, all the better! We need Christian community—church gatherings, small groups, meetings, discipling relationships, and friendships. But we may also need counselors, therapists, and medical professionals who can be conduits for a tangible healing experience with the Great Physician that leaves us not only cured but whole. Having Jesus and a therapist too isn't a lack of faith, it's wisdom. And in my experience on both sides of the counselor's

---

18. "Study of Acute Mental Illness and Christian Faith," LifeWay Research, September 2014, lifewayresearch.com/wp-content/uploads/2014/09/Acute-Mental-Illness-and-Christian-Faith-Research-Report-1.pdf.

chair, God can reveal powerful truths about identity in counseling that can heal parts of our lives we didn't even know were broken.

GOD CAN REVEAL POWERFUL TRUTHS ABOUT IDENTITY IN COUNSELING THAT CAN HEAL PARTS OF OUR LIVES WE DIDN'T EVEN KNOW WERE BROKEN.

When one of us struggles, we all struggle. When one of us falls, we all fall. Whether we want to believe it or not, we *are all one in Christ Jesus*" (Galatians 3:28). I believe embracing vulnerability and destigmatizing therapy and intervention in the church will spark a revival that will overflow into the secular recovery space like wildfire. It's an untapped well of evangelistic grace that could show the whole world how loved and forgiven they really are—by God and by us. We're called to create safe places where people can come as they are and leave better than they were. It's what God does—because of who He is. He's a good Father.

The time has come to bridge the gap between Spirit and science in the recovery space. And we, the church, must be willing to make the first move in grace and love. Our mindsets, drivers, and approaches will be different. But we need each other to bring reform in the recovery space. At the heart of it all, both camps want the same thing—to see people struggling with addiction, mental health problems, and suicidal thoughts break free and live fuller, more abundant lives. Imagine what we could learn from one another! We can do exponentially more together, working as one, united in our cause. And when we, the church, can lay down our pride and bridge the gap? The whole world will want to know what—or more appropriately, *Who*—it is we carry.

I believe healing and curing are both of God. They put His goodness on display and create a hope-filled wonder about His character and our identity. He is a good Father who wants good things for us, His children and coheirs to the kingdom with Jesus. Our full inheritance is available to us right now. God's will is that we are healed of all wounds and cured of all diseases so that our hearts can be made whole and our lives can be transformed by the power of the Holy Spirit. Sobriety, whether it comes through healing or curing, isn't our end game. Transformation is the ultimate goal, and a promised-land life worth staying sober for is the destination.

The impossibly difficult part about having transformation as the ultimate goal in recovery is that sometimes we don't quite see the healing and curing we expected. One of our former residents, Mike McCoy, had one of these stories. Mike was a scary dude. Underneath his permanent scowl and prison-sculpted physique, Mike's heart and mind housed a lifetime of trauma and abuse. As a young boy, he watched as three black men raped and murdered his mother. The confusion of this experience left him violently racist and addicted to any and every escape he could find.

To make matters even worse, Mike came to us with severe diabetes that caused terrifying seizures and put our community at risk. Many inpatient facilities wouldn't take Mike in because he was so dangerous, but we knew the moment we met him that he was already part of our family.

Mike's heart, mind, and life were completely transformed in a year and a half with the Timothy Initiative. He was able to safely process his trauma and racist tendencies without judgment, and he was introduced to God as a good Father for the first time in his life. The grace he received for his reprehensible actions toward people of color in the past moved him to love more deeply in our diverse inner-city Tampa community. He bought gifts for Haitian children in our neighborhood and became a powerful voice of racial reconciliation for our ministry. Yet even with a heart and life transformation that was nothing short of miraculous, Mike's diabetes continued to wage war against his body. Doctors faithfully explored every possible avenue, but they were convinced that the disease would blind Mike and eventually kill him. We were thankful for their intervention and wisdom, but we kept believing with Mike for total healing of his diabetic episodes. After a lifetime of abusing himself and others, he was finally free, and we couldn't imagine his life ending now. Mike no longer feared hell—but he was eager to live as much of his promised-land life as possible.

God's ways are mysterious. After a long battle, Mike passed away in our care, completely sober and reconciled to his past. The total healing cure we believed for never came. There are days I still struggle to understand why. But the transformation in Mike's life was evident to all and celebrated by everyone he knew. He lived a promised-land life that represented the grace-filled heart of the Father. This is the greatest gift we can ever hope to give people in recovery. And it's the reason why we value total life transformation over baseline sobriety *every single time*.

WHERE SPIRIT AND SCIENCE MEET

From Genesis all the way through Revelation, God is on a mission, reconciling the whole world back to Himself. (See 2 Corinthians 5:19.) It starts in the garden of Eden just after Adam and Eve ate of the Tree of the Knowledge of Good and Evil, bringing sin into the perfect world God had made for them. Instead of responding in anger, as many well-meaning preachers would retell the tale, He responds with the heart of a good and loving Father eager to know who convinced His children they weren't *already* like Him. He asks, *"Who told you that you were naked?"* (Genesis 3:11). Brokenhearted, He made garments for Adam and Eve, clothed them, and ushered them out of the garden. Had they continued to eat from the garden's Tree of Life, they would have been doomed to an eternal state of sin.

Throughout the generations, God fought to get His people to return to Him. He made the Law, but we couldn't (and oftentimes wouldn't) follow it faithfully. He destroyed evil by water in the flood and fire at Sodom and Gomorrah, but more sin manifested. God finally decided to destroy our sin for us—by becoming sin in and through the shed blood of Jesus. Now that sin has been defeated, the Father wants us to know how loved, forgiven, and free we already are so we can step into the fullness of the promised-land life He has for all of us. This is radical reconciliation.

The recovery space should be no different—and yet, we remain divided. With both sacred and secular camps clinging to their convictions, we've come to see one another as *the other* at best and *the enemy* at worst. This rigid, competitive dichotomy between Spirit and science results in major missed opportunities for those who feel a call to help people struggling with addiction, mental health problems, and suicidal thoughts. We're more interested in being right than being effective.

The key to breakthrough in recovery on all sides lies just beyond the walls we've built. As much as we'd like to believe it, we, the church, don't have all the answers. God is breaking through in medical science on a daily basis, and a big portion of the church is missing out.

Conversely, medical scientists who rely solely on what can be seen and proven may be missing out on the very real yet unseen elements that supernaturally move people beyond baseline sobriety into transformation territory. We, the church, need what the scientific community has to share with us. Conversely, the scientific community needs the intangible hope we've found. I firmly believe co-laboring with people of different belief systems does not have to compromise our own convictions. When we approach one another with open hearts and willing hands, we witness true breakthrough.

I'm honored to participate on an interfaith alliance of recovery leaders in the greater Tampa area called the Community & Faith Leaders Coalition. Through open forums, panel discussions, and safe, healthy dialogue, Christian, atheist, Buddhist, Muslim, and agnostic recovery specialists who are counselors, ministers, doctors, lawmakers, and advocates have an opportunity to share insights, swap stories, and develop better strategies by learning from and with one another. In these diverse circles, I have found some of our greatest ministry allies—partners, donors, and volunteers who are themselves transformed by being in relationship with our radical community of Jesus people. They don't always understand what—or *Who*—we carry, but they know they want to be a part of it.

> WHEN WE APPROACH ONE ANOTHER WITH OPEN HEARTS AND WILLING HANDS, WE WITNESS TRUE BREAKTHROUGH.

So to the scientific professionals who have picked up this book, thank you. You've acknowledged the benefits and efforts of faith communities in recovery, and we are grateful. We humbly ask that you educate, empower, and support our collective efforts. Continue to advocate for therapy and medication that will contribute to healing and wholeness. Invite us into what it might mean to find a cure—we will meet you there. And please, if there's more you'd like to know about the intangible elements of our faith that support the healing journey, all you need to do is ask.

And to the faith-based recovery leaders who have picked up this book, thank you. There's been a lot of tough love laid down in these pages, especially toward the Christian recovery community. And yet, here you are—still reading. The Uncovery is a call for people of faith to eagerly engage with the clinicians, mental health professionals, and other members of the secular recovery community to discover new ways we might come alongside people in recovery. It's time to break through the walls of the manmade church and come together to care with some of the most brilliant minds on earth. It's time to honor the divine DNA in all people and graciously invite them into what our communities are uncovering—inner healing, deliverance ministries, and more. Don't try to convince people of anything. Just invite, honor, listen, and learn until the Holy Spirit prompts you to say or do something more. Trust me, He will. Who knows? You might even get to share the gospel while you're at it.

QUESTIONS FOR REFLECTION

1. What does healing mean to you?

_____

_____

_____

_____

2. Do you believe there is room for the Holy Spirit and science in the recovery process? Why or why not?

_____

_____

_____

_____

3. Is God prompting you to do *something more* in your recovery ministry? If so, what?

_____

_____

_____

_____

7

SYSTEMATIZING VS. CULTIVATING

"I have the right to do anything," you say—but not
everything is beneficial. "I have the right to do anything"—
but not everything is constructive.
No one should seek their own good, but the good of others.
—1 Corinthians 10:23–24

In the early days of the Christian church, things were tough but simple. Our commission was clear: *"Go and make disciples of all nations, baptizing them in the name of the Father and of the Son and of the Holy Spirit"* (Matthew 28:19). Nobody asked if they would be *able* to do this—they simply looked with compassion on a broken world and asked God *how* to reach them.

On the day of Pentecost, confusion turned into conviction as believers were filled with the Holy Spirit and answered the call. There were no megachurches, no elaborate giving campaigns, no concrete campus expansion strategies, and no hardcore set of rules and regulations on how to *do church* beyond the life of Jesus, the voice of the Spirit, and the emerging letters of Paul to new-convert congregations around the world. Early Christians simply devoted themselves to the apostles' teaching, fellowship, communion, and prayer. (See Acts 2:42.) And in its radically simple conviction, the

Acts 2 church plant spread like grassroots wildfire throughout the region, and people came to Jesus in droves.

If we've learned anything about the remnants of the first-century church in the twenty-first century, it's that more of a good thing isn't always a good thing. This is especially true when it comes to recovery. The megachurch movement of the 1980s and 1990s made Jesus more attractive and more accessible for modern times, but the manmade model was volume over value. This *big church* movement left us with outreach, discipleship, and recovery programs that not only don't work but are bleeding the church dry. Jesus never took a cookie-cutter approach, so why would we? We need less one-size-fits-all programming and more one-on-one authentic relationships to provide less systematizing and more cultivating.

> THE BIG CHURCH MOVEMENT LEFT US WITH OUTREACH, DISCIPLESHIP, AND RECOVERY PROGRAMS THAT NOT ONLY DON'T WORK BUT ARE BLEEDING THE CHURCH DRY.

Generations X and Y—those born from 1965 to 1980, and 1981 to 1996, respectively—are increasingly disenchanted and disenfranchised with the modern church. So are their children and grandchildren, Gen Z and Gen A. But many of them haven't yet given up on their faith. In fact, they are growing increasingly fascinated with the ideals and persona of Christ, but they want nothing to do with people who call themselves Christian yet don't act much like Jesus at all.

Respected Hindu leader Mahatma Gandhi revered Jesus and quoted Him often. Missionary E. Stanley Jones once asked the gentle spirited man, "Mr. Gandhi, though you quote the words of Christ often, why is that you appear to so adamantly reject becoming his follower?" Gandhi's reply was sobering. "Oh, I don't reject your Christ. I love your Christ. It is just that so many of you Christians are so unlike your Christ."[19]

Gandhi would know. When he was a young man practicing law in South Africa, he studied the Bible and the teachings of Jesus, exploring the idea of becoming a Christian. Until he decided to attend a church service. As he approached the building entrance, a church elder stopped him in his tracks. "Where do you think you're going, kaffir?"[20] His offensive, racial slur made it clear Gandhi wasn't welcome. From that traumatic moment on, Gandhi affirmed and adopted the good he saw in Christ but knew he could never be a part of the Christian church.

Trauma doesn't always bring about addiction, but all addiction stems from trauma. It's important for recovery leaders to better understand the racial implications of trauma. Most leaders in the Christian church and Christian recovery circles are white men. This is not a criticism, it's just reality. When we invite people of color into recovery programming that is predominantly white-male dominated, past trauma can create perceived barriers to entry. While most recovery leaders can't fathom the idea of stopping a person of color at the door with ethnic slurs, we must also acknowledge that they may not feel safe in our circles.

I know this to be true even in inner-city Tampa, Florida— white men like me are the minority, and yet we see very few people of color come to us through the Timothy Initiative. It's not because they don't *need* help. It's because even in our radically grace-filled community, they still don't feel like they could ever really belong because of the personal and generational trauma they've experienced. Working through and overcoming this deep-seated trauma requires authentic relationships and unapologetic advocacy.

---

19. "Gandhi's message to Christians," Gandhian Institutions, www.mkgandhi. org/africaneedsgandhi/ gandhis_message_to_christians.php.
20. Ibid.

MICROAGGRESSION MEETS CHRISTIAN NATIONALISM

If you're a particularly "woke" white person, you may already be thinking about how to better show up as an advocate for people of color. But even if you think you're ready, you might still have some work to do. People I love and do active ministry with in the Christian community still cringe when they hear terms like *white privilege* and aggressively combat the phrase "black lives matter" with the response, "All lives matter." The subtle microaggression and obvious macroaggression people of color feel is something we, the church, must learn to recognize, own, and remedy, even if we can never fully understand how it feels to walk in their shoes. If not us, then who? If not now, then when?

Macroaggressions are deliberate, blatantly damaging acts of discrimination on a systemic level that hurt certain groups at the individual level. Historic macroaggressions include the forced relocation of Japanese-Americans into internment camps during World War II and the Tuskegee study in which black men were intentionally misled and denied standard treatment for syphilis.[21] Today, we see macroaggression when employers reject job applicants whose names *sound funny*, those expressing hatred for all Chinese because of COVID-19, or corporations that intentionally jack up prices at stores in *certain neighborhoods*.

These blatant episodes are perhaps even less dangerous than the *microaggression* people of color feel—the things white people might never even notice, let alone fight against.

Case in point? Band-Aids. Historically, nearly all adhesive bandages were peach-colored, reminding people of color that they're different with every wound. This microaggression is just one example of systemic racism that white people don't have to think about. Interestingly, in the wake of widespread racial unrest

21. Brandon M. Togioka et al., "Diversity and Discrimination In Healthcare," StatPearls Publishing LLC, August 25, 2021, www.ncbi.nlm.nih.gov/books/NBK568721.

in 2020, Band-Aid Brand Adhesive Bandages announced that it would expand its predominantly pink-hued product line to produce a range of bandages that "embrace the beauty of diverse skin," including light, medium, and deep shades of brown and black skin tones. Band-Aid tried this before in 2005, but that line was "discontinued due to lack of interest at the time."[22]

Some individuals exhibit microaggression without even realizing it. For instance, telling an American-born Latino, "You speak excellent English," or telling a black man, "You're a credit to your race." These backhanded compliments are really insults.

My colors are clear: If you're not for people of color in your community, you're against them. Even after years of intentional progress and honest effort, we, the church, *still* struggle to recognize racial trauma and show appropriate compassion in the communities we're called to serve. And I believe we're losing generations of would-be believers because of it. Try as we may, we still don't look much like Jesus at all.

> DIFFERENT CIRCUMSTANCES IMPACT DIFFERENT PEOPLE IN DIFFERENT WAYS FOR DIFFERENT REASONS—WHICH IS WHY WE HAVE NO ROOM TO JUDGE WHAT TRIGGERS TRAUMA INSIDE ANOTHER PERSON.

Trauma is more than just something that happens to a person on the outside. Trauma is what happens *inside* of a person as a result of what happens to them. Different circumstances impact different people in different ways for different reasons—which is why we have no room to judge what triggers trauma inside another person. The eye-opening, trauma-filled perspectives of other

22. Julia Naftulin, "Band-Aid will make bandages in a wider range of skin tones, but some people say it took far too long," *Insider*, June 12, 2020, www.insider.com/band-aid-wider-range-skin-tones-took-too-long-2020-6.

religious leaders such as Gandhi might be enough to make us reconsider our approach to nonbelievers and new believers alike.

This transcends race, of course. Discrimination and marginalization because of age, gender, religion, disability, sexual orientation or identity, socioeconomic status, mental health, and addiction are issues Christian recovery leaders cannot afford to ignore or avoid. Now, I'm not advocating for some new brand of universalism that rejects the truth of God's Word. Far from it. You can—and must—have courage in your convictions. What we also need to adopt is *compassion* in our convictions. Jesus never glossed over people who were on the margins of society. It didn't matter how they got there. He welcomed them, walked with them, broke bread with them, and left them completely transformed.

This topic hits home for me in a big way. Julie and I have an amazing transgender son, Finn, who we would love to be able to invite to church. The problem is, Finn doesn't see church as a place where he could ever be welcome. He could be one step away from a transformative encounter with Jesus, someone he grew up knowing as a friend of sinners. But at this point on his journey, Finn wants nothing to do with Jesus because of the way so-called Christians have treated him and the LGBTQ community as a whole. He doesn't need some watered-down version of the gospel that says, "Anything goes." He needs people to welcome him, walk with him, break bread with him, and create space for him to have a transformative encounter with Jesus, who was a friend to sinners. But it's possible to be so right that we, the church, are actually *wrong* in the hate-filled, abusive ways we walk out our faith.

Contrary to popular opinion, it *is* possible to stand for truth and do it in love. It's also quite possible to be so *right* you're actually wrong, using Scripture to back your anti-Christ assertions. If it's not the truth, it's not loving. And if it's not loving, it's not the truth. Sometimes a look in the mirror is all it takes. Lutheran pastor, theologian, and anti-Nazi dissident Dietrich Bonhoeffer's prophetic words warned the church against the negative effects of Christian nationalism long before big church as we know it came to be.

> The messengers of Jesus will be hated to the end of time. They will be blamed for all the divisions which rend cities and homes. Jesus and his disciples will be condemned on all sides for undermining family life, and for leading the nation astray; they will be called crazy fanatics and disturbers of the peace. The disciples will be sorely tempted to desert their Lord. But the end is also near, and they must hold on and persevere until it comes. Only he will be blessed who remains loyal to Jesus and his word until the end.[23]

The knowledge that we'll be hated and misunderstood does not dismiss our call to oneness in Christ. Bonhoeffer loved to quote Psalm 133, proving that our call to unity can only be fully embraced when we can fight and remain standing with one another and for one another. Do we know how to stand together as one, indivisible, even in our disagreement?

> *How good and pleasant it is when God's people live together in unity!* It is like precious oil poured on the head, running down on the beard, running down on Aaron's beard, down on the collar of his robe. It is as if the dew of Hermon were falling on Mount Zion. For there the LORD bestows his blessing, even life forevermore.   (Psalm 133:1–3)

A UNIFIED APPROACH TO RELAPSE

Unity manifests in everything we do at the Timothy Initiative, especially when it comes to relapse. Instead of a violation of

---

23. Dietrich Bonhoeffer, *The Cost of Discipleship* (New York: Macmillan Publishing Co., 1979), 239.

guidelines resulting in discrimination, dismissal, or excommunication, it prompts us to go even deeper with the ones we love and lead through the Uncovery. When relapse happens, I ask our T.I. brothers four critical questions—and I never accept, "I don't know" or "Just because" as final answers.

1. WHAT HAPPENED?

People don't relapse because they want to. More often than not, relapse is brought about by a trigger that exists because of trauma. Retracing steps to find out what led to the trigger and why that trigger exists in the first place can bring clarity and hope.

2. WHAT'S REALLY GOING ON?

Just as outbursts are *never about the dishes*, relapses are rarely if ever what they seem from an external view. Gaining a deeper understanding of the emotional and mental health of the person who relapsed can provide insights for healthier boundaries and stronger levels of accountability and healing.

3. WHAT DO YOU WANT TO DO NOW?

Handing down punishments and slapping on additional restrictions when someone relapses is like rubbing salt in a wound. Instead, allow them to consciously choose to remain in community and help them set realistic and sustainable limits for themselves that will help them move toward transformation.

4. WHAT DO YOU NEED FROM ME?

This question elicits some funny responses, but it's the most important one you can ask if you want to walk with people on their Uncovery journeys. They may not want to ask for your help. They may not yet know they even need your help. But offering support in this way shows compassion and proof that you're willing to stand with them and be there for them, even when they stumble.

They may not remember what you said or did, but they'll always remember how you made them feel.

We, the church, will be sorely misunderstood on our best days, and hated on our worst. We'll not only be misunderstood *as* the church, but we'll be also misunderstood *by* the church. Some will see us as hate-filled and bigoted; others will think we're greasy-grace dealers and false prophets. Are you willing to do whatever God asks of you, with little regard for what the world—or the church—thinks of you?

THE JOY THAT GOES BEFORE US AND SUSTAINS US CAN DRIVE US TO TAKE TERRITORY FOR THE KINGDOM IF WE REMAIN SENSITIVE TO THE VOICE OF THE HOLY SPIRIT.

The burden that comes with spreading the gospel is real, but the joy that goes before us and sustains us can drive us to take territory for the kingdom—if, and only if, we remain sensitive to the voice of the Holy Spirit. Manmade models of Christendom continue to crumble as more and more people reject the church. And yet, our commission remains clear: *"Go and make disciples"* (Matthew 28:19). We don't need another system, another process, or another step-by-step series to make it happen. We need nothing more than the simple gospel and hearts transformed by Grace Himself.

When I first began sharing the concept of the Uncovery with trusted friends and advisors, I knew I had a big problem. "I know you keep saying people don't need another twelve-step program," one told me. "But the problem is, people *like* to buy programs." I know she's right. Systems and models are easier. People like to know exactly what to do so they can check a box and be done. As I tried to reconcile this with what I know I heard from God, the Uncovery has evolved into what I call the *anti-model*. While we're not coming against traditional recovery programming, we are inviting leaders to break the mold and ask God, "What more can be done?"

God speaks to each person so differently. What He asks of me may not look anything like what He asks of you. That's why surefire steps and easy answers just don't exist in the Uncovery. It's more like stepping into the wilderness with God, all-in, promised-land life or bust. But if we are fellow travelers on a journey, staying faithful to how we've been called, I believe we can all accomplish more together than we ever could on our own—far more than if we all showed up to help in the exact same way. More of a good thing is only a good thing when God is the One driving it, not you or me.

MASS PRODUCTION AND ASSIMILATION

We, the church, are notorious for trying to *build* what God wants to *grow*. Fulfilling the Great Commission certainly takes some level of community organization. We call it *the church*, but those words mean different things to different people. Although organization is not inherently bad, God wants to bless the *organism* of the church, brought to life in the hearts and minds of those who love and fear Him. This is what will faithfully carry forth the Great Commission. The question isn't whether it will happen—it's how it will happen. And it's those precious few who are rooted in intimacy with the Father who will know their positions on the front lines. Like stealth agents, they give God their *yes* before they even know what He asks of them.

STEALTH AGENTS LIKE ME AREN'T ALWAYS APPRECIATED BY THE REST OF THE CHURCH THAT'S STILL LITERALLY AND FIGURATIVELY HOLDING DOWN THE FORT.

When God asked me to start the Timothy Initiative, I quickly learned that stealth agents like me aren't always appreciated by the rest of the church that's still literally and figuratively holding down the fort. In attempts to articulate the anti-model through faith-based fundraising efforts, ministry partnerships, and cross-denominational conversations, the response was often, "Yeah, we already have AA on Wednesday nights," or "I don't know, that sounds a little too risky."

Most faith communities preferred a white-picket-fence program approach to recovery with endless happily-ever-afters, achieved through a predictable model with tangible results. I didn't have it. What rose to the surface more than anything else was a scarcity-driven, competitive spirit that silently screamed, "Oh, so you think you can do better than us? Good luck!"

I confess this rejection stirred anger in me that I carried for the first six years of my ministry. With each success, I wanted to throw it back in the faces of those who doubted what I heard from God. I was tempted to withhold my discoveries, even when people humbly asked what we were learning with repentant and curious hearts. But when I finally had a breakdown after my brother's death, the people who surrounded me and my ministry were the ones I never thought would have my back. Traditional churches with traditional recovery programing stepped up. Faith-based inpatient rehab teams and even secular medical professionals surrounded and loved me. Even though they were called differently than I was, they knew me as a man on a mission to help people break free from addiction and build promised-land lives. For the first time ever, I realized how much we all needed each other, and that our unity didn't require agreement on everything.

As cross-denominational and interfaith collaboration has grown over the years with the Timothy Initiative and the Sober Truth Project, authentic relationships have grown, too. Stepping into the unknown through the Uncovery has been incredibly fruitful, with people like Mike, Joe, and others to affirm with their testimony that different isn't always bad. We've created safe places for people to better understand the true nature and character of God.

Big church, and big recovery by proxy, have done wonderful things to raise awareness of the need for what we're doing through the Uncovery—going after the people who fall through the cracks in whatever way God asks us to. It's from this place of intimacy with one another and with God that we can determine our next steps. And those steps will rarely if ever mean duplication or assimilation. They will be as unique as grapes on a vine, flowers in a field, or snowflakes on the windowsill. They may carry similarities, but no two are exactly the same.

Building something with a blueprint is simple and satisfying, at least on a surface level. Cultivating a new garden of Eden through the Uncovery with God is far more conceptual—but for those who are called to it, it can be far more fruitful and rewarding in the context of eternity. Know your calling. Own your season. And discern the voice of your Father as He leads you out of your comfort zone and into the unknown.

THE RELIGION OF RECOVERY

Real recovery requires intimate relationship with God and people. This is where traditional recovery can break down, especially when it's developed or implemented with a religious spirit— when it values the belief system of faith and worship more than the individual and values box-checking over transformation. The Uncovery reveals our true identity and dismisses that box-checking religious spirit. When that happens, our identity solidifies, and we grow closer to God and hear from God more clearly. In order to transform, people need to be taught how to hear from God independently—without a leader interpreting God's voice and doing the work for them. Even if you commit to be with them on their recovery journey, they won't be able to rely on you forever.

In general, the Christian religious spirit condemns, while the person of Jesus shows compassion. And when we, the church, try to walk out the Great Commission, we too often do it from a place of religion than a place of relationship. You can't have a relationship with a belief. You can only have a relationship with a person. The reason I believe Gandhi struggled to follow Jesus is because he was conditioned to look for a religion, not a relationship. And when a religious spirit reared its ugly head at that South African church, we lost a good man who loved Christ but wanted nothing to do with His people. As Christian recovery leaders, we have much to learn from the mistakes of our churches. The shaming and blaming we're known for has fostered a perceived need for anonymity because struggling people fear they will no longer be welcome if they're not living religiously.

> WE WANT TO LEARN HOW TO WALK VULNERABLY THROUGH OUR STRUGGLES AS OUR MINDS AND HEARTS ARE RENEWED BY GOD'S LOVE THROUGH HIS PEOPLE.

But what if the recovery arm of the church changed the narrative? What if instead of boxes to check, steps to take, and rules to follow, we created a safe environment for people to encounter the real God and grow organically in relationship with Him? The very nature of the word *Uncovery* implies getting to the root of our struggles with addiction, mental health, and suicidal thoughts. We don't want to be labeled by them or hide underneath them; we want to learn how to walk vulnerably through our struggles as our minds and hearts are renewed by God's love through His people. No more hiding, no more shaming, and no more blaming. Just love.

THE HUMAN ELEMENT

No matter what our backgrounds, religious affiliations, political persuasions, or lifestyles, we humans can usually agree on one thing—we need each other. We are wired for connection and without it, we will not thrive. Our need for the human element in all we do stems from how we were created to be in relationship with God and other people.

During the Vietnam War, young, able-bodied American men were taken from their homes, given a license to kill, and shipped off to fight in a war they barely understood. It's no surprise that in the face of abject confusion, trauma, and loss, many of those men became addicted to heroin while fighting overseas. The widespread availability of the drug and our soldiers' understandable desire to escape reality birthed what should have been a drug epidemic in post-war America. And yet, when they came home, very few of the soldiers who abused heroin during their combat season remained addicted after the war. In fact, 95 percent quit cold turkey and stayed in remission.[24] Why? How? Because they had family, friends, and a promised-land life to come home to and stay sober for. Life certainly wasn't simple thereafter, but these men, removed from what was undoubtedly the most stress-filled situation of their lives, were better in community.

> WE NEED TO BE BRAVE ENOUGH TO ASK, "WHY THE PAIN?"
> AND "WHAT ARE YOU RUNNING FROM?"

This example makes the case for asking questions that go deeper than, "Why do you have this addiction?" We need to be brave enough to ask, "Why the pain?" and "What are you running

---

24. Lee N. Robins et al., "How Permanent Was Vietnam Drug Addiction?", *American Journal of Public Health*, December 1, 1974, www.ncbi.nlm.nih.gov/pmc/articles/PMC1775687.

from?" We were never meant to go it alone—in faith, in recovery, or in life. And since the fall, God has been moving heaven and earth to bring us back into right relationship with Him again. We are the hands and feet of this grace movement and a powerful force for the kingdom of God in a collective human element. More often than not, people encounter God through other people. The burden of responsibility here is huge—and our one and only job is to represent the Father's heart.

With the spiritually diverse nature of the people I'm called to co-labor with in recovery circles, I occasionally get criticism about my own brand of Christianity being too soft. My grace comes off a little too greasy for comfort, and I sure don't look, speak, or act much like a pastor. I'm sure these observations come from a place of tough love and people trying to help me better assimilate into a religious system. But I take the negative feedback as affirmation that I'm right on point with God's call on this season of my life. If my ministry looked anything like the traditional church, the people I'm called to love and lead through the Uncovery would never see me as a safe person to confide in.

Jesus sure didn't look, speak, or act like the rabbis of His day. He may not have had sleeves of tattoos and ripped jeans like I have, but He certainly knew how to invite sinners into relationship and bring transformative salvation to their houses. Jesus gave grace so freely, it got Him killed. And by that same grace, He triumphed over sin and death and saved us all.

Now, I'm not Jesus. The very thought of that makes me laugh out loud. But I know the risen Jesus lives in me by the power of the Holy Spirit—and because of that, I'm one with Him and the Father. This leaves me in awe of the authority I carry and humbled to the point of complete obedience to whatever God asks of me. And so, to the best of my ability, I only say what God is saying and I only do what God is doing.

I know you need me to say it plainly, so here you go:

True transformational recovery doesn't work without Jesus.

I keep unusually diverse company in my ministry ranks, but I am unapologetic about the source of the transformative power we carry together: Jesus. Only Jesus. You can't spend more than ten minutes hanging out with me without the goodness of God washing over the conversation. It's like breathing for me. And yet, while I always feared this would be a barrier to finding support outside of faith communities, I find my secular collaborators are drawn to the Jesus in me. They may not always understand or agree with my religious views, but they want to know more about what—or more appropriately, *Who*—I carry. To this day, I've never lost a collaborator by being 100 percent sold-out for my King, Jesus. Whether God is moving through Spirit, science, or a beautiful blend of both, I give God the glory in everything I do.

THE HARVEST IS RIPE

Leading Christian recovery as stewards, not owners, requires organic intentionality. This happens when we stop trying to *build* what God wants to *grow*, allowing Him to cultivate *"a new thing"* (Isaiah 43:19) in our hearts and lives. As Jesus told His disciples, *"The harvest is plentiful but the workers are few"* (Matthew 9:37). It's time for all of us to go a level deeper in how we love and lead our recovery communities. In my own journey, this means staying in tune to the needs of the Timothy Initiative and Sober Truth Project, showing up for my people in a way that's authentic, vulnerable, and safe. The same applies in your recovery communities, too.

BEING YOUR BROTHER'S KEEPER MEANS YOU WILL NEED TO BE WILLING TO CHANGE THE WAY YOU DO LIFE WITH AND LOVE THEM.

Paul makes this clear when he says, *"All food is clean, but it is wrong for a person to eat anything that causes someone else to stumble"* (Romans 14:20). Admittedly, he's talking about meat. You die-hard theologians may be rolling your eyes, but the lesson still applies! Being your brother's keeper means you will, without a doubt, need to be willing to change the way you do life with and love them. If a friend or family member struggles with alcohol, you may need to abstain from it in their presence to acknowledge, celebrate, and support their sobriety. If your spouse is struggling with mental health, you may need to carry your vows on your chest—for better or worse, in sickness or in health, to choose to love when others would flee. If a co-worker is struggling with suicidal thoughts, you may need to cross typical work boundaries to make a deeper connection and be available to help them get the support they need.

If God requires something more of you—something that goes beyond a system, a model, a guideline, or a program of the day—are you willing to say yes? If so, you've entered into Uncovery territory.

So whether you eat or drink or whatever you do, do it all for the glory of God. Do not cause anyone to stumble, whether Jews, Greeks or the church of God—even as I try to please everyone in every way. For I am not seeking my own good but the good of many, so that they may be saved.

(1 Corinthians 10:31–33)

QUESTIONS FOR REFLECTION

1. How might knowing about trauma in someone's life help you love them well in recovery?

_____

_____

_____

_____

2. Do you identify more with the idea of being a captive or a prisoner? Why?

_____

_____

_____

_____

3. Do you believe transformational recovery can happen without Jesus? Why or why not?

_____

_____

_____

_____

PART III

REPOSITIONING RECOVERY

Christian recovery can be an isolating space for leaders and lay-people alike. The pressure to help people struggling with addiction, mental health problems, and suicidal thoughts to assimilate into church culture and get better for good is overwhelming. It can be easy to forget the commission we carry—*"Go and make disciples of all nations, baptizing them in the name of the Father and of the Son and of the Holy Spirit"* (Matthew 28:19)—because we're so freaking busy fixing people, or at least making sure they don't make a scene. Why are we doing this anyway? Why lead recovery, why do it in the context of the church, and why now—when people are walking away from Christendom faster and more furiously than ever before?

I believe recovery is the key to the abundant life Jesus came to give humankind. For people who struggle—and if we're honest, we know we all do—recovery is life. Recovery is the most powerful tool at our disposal for advancing the gospel and a ticket to revival like we've never seen before. A new generation of hope-filled believers is about to rise up from the ashes through the Uncovery and win generations to come for Jesus. Will you be one of them?

8

RECOVERY AND LIFE

Healing is not the resolution of our past;
it is the use of our past to draw us into deeper
relationship with God and his purposes for our lives.
—Dan B. Allender

If you can breathe, you can hurt. Even the most abundant lives are filled with heartache and disappointment. Pain is part of what makes us human. And as humans—especially as Christians—we struggle to accept this reality, let alone deal with it in healthy and productive ways.

Countless instances in Scripture promise the reality of pain in our lives. God's most beloved sons and daughters experienced unthinkable pain and loss, not to mention some of the most horrific *deaths* in history. Even Jesus, God in the flesh, wasn't exempt from the problem of pain in this life. And rather than trying to convince people out of their pain as we often do, He met them smack in the middle of it. He wept with them and prayed with them, never pitching false promises or empty platitudes. He gave it to 'em straight.

Case in point, in the Gospel of John, when Jesus tried to explain to His disciples that He would soon be leaving them—sparing them the details of the horrific and painful crucifixion He would experience to triumph over sin and death—they could barely wrap their minds around the thought of losing Him, even if it might be for their own good and His glory.

> *Very truly I tell you, you will weep and mourn while the world rejoices. You will grieve, but your grief will turn to joy. A woman giving birth to a child has pain because her time has come; but when her baby is born she forgets the anguish because of her joy that a child is born into the world. So with you: Now is your time of grief, but I will see you again and you will rejoice, and no one will take away your joy.*
>   (John 16:20–22)

The disciples responded to Jesus's quite literal self-fulfilling prophecy as we might have—with great confusion. They couldn't fathom how life could ever be better without Jesus right there with them in the flesh, and the thought of it was more than they could bear. "What do you mean You're leaving? We're only three years into this ministry! How could you do this to us, Jesus?"

The coming anguish, loss, and isolation their rabbi and friend foretold just didn't make any earthly sense. But Jesus's implication of direct access to God the Father—something only Jesus had up to that point—kept their attention. His next words hung awkwardly in the balance.

> *Though I have been speaking figuratively, a time is coming when I will no longer use this kind of language but will tell you plainly about my Father. In that day you will ask in my name. I am not saying that I will ask the Father on your behalf. No, the Father himself loves you because you have loved me and have believed that I came from God. I came from the Father and entered the world; now I am leaving the world and going back to the Father.*   (John 16:25–28)

The disciples would have been hard-pressed to argue with Jesus at this point. He spoke clearly, with no metaphors, parables, or veiled figures of speech. They may not have liked the promise of pain in His words, but they could cling to the promise of hope Jesus also made plain.

> *I have told you these things, so that in me you may have peace.* **In this world you will have trouble.** *But take heart!* **I have overcome the world.** (John 16:33)

Pain and trauma will be part of life. It was true for the disciples, and it's true for every believer and would-be believer who walks the earth. But I believe if we, the church, could change the narrative around pain, we could help people leverage it to build promised-land lives—not only for themselves but for others, too.

> PAIN CAN EITHER DESTROY US OR USHER US INTO OUR BEST LIVES. BUT INSTEAD OF CONVINCING PEOPLE OUT OF OR AROUND THEIR SUFFERING, WHAT IF WE WALKED WITH THEM THROUGH IT?

Pain can either destroy us or usher us into our best lives. Ultimately, the individual heart will decide. But instead of convincing people out of or around their suffering, what if we walked with them through it? What if we allowed people to experience pain as a refining fire to bring clarity and purpose? If people are meant to meet Jesus along a path of suffering, only to be introduced to a loving Father God who wants to heal their life and restore their joy, who are we to stand in the way?

All too often, we, the church, rob people of these precious refining seasons through religious manipulation and spiritual ultimatums. And the worst part is, we're so conditioned to it, we don't even realize we're doing it. We downplay trauma. We ignore abuse. We cover up sin and allow room for marginalization and discrimination. We bully suffering souls into believing that their pain would just go away if they simply had enough faith. We convince bound and broken brothers and sisters that they can be free and whole if they'll just repent and check our boxes. We stay on the surface, avoid the hard questions, and speak in maddening circles to make sure everything stays okay or at least *looks* okay in case anyone important questions it.

This is why people hide. This is why people fall. This is why people run from God the Father instead of toward Him. It's on us. And we, the church, thanks to the Holy Spirit within us, have both the power and the responsibility to change the conversation.

THE LANGUAGE OF RECOVERY

I've learned many lessons the hard way in over a decade of recovery ministry. The hardest of those lessons is this sobering truth: Once someone has made up their mind about something, there's no *convincing* them out of it. There just aren't enough compelling *reasons* why they should stay sober, mentally stable, or even alive once they have decided on an opposite course of action. Guilt and shame won't change it. Rules and regulations won't either. Powerful arguments and generous incentives amount to nothing in our own strength. The only lasting hope we have to seek and save the lost is divine intervention from the Father through the Spirit.

For some of you, this may sound like Christianity 101. If it's no longer I who live but Christ who lives within me (see Galatians 2:20), then it should be easy to *"live and move and have [my] being"* (Acts 17:28) as a beloved child of God the Father, right? The truth is, even God-revering, Jesus-loving, Holy Spirit-led believers will still wrestle in their own strength until every one of us walks with a Jacob limp! Fulfilling the Great Commission in our thoughts, words, and actions requires a level of invitation, challenge, sensitivity, and nuance that few are teaching these days.

When I train recovery leaders through the Timothy Initiative, the Sober Truth Project, and other recovery ministries, language and tone often come up as they relate to people struggling with suicidal thoughts. When a person has decided to take their own life, there is little to nothing we can say or do in our own strength to change their minds. We can only intervene when someone is still on the edge of indecision about suicide, when they may be thinking about it and even longing for it but haven't resolved to take action on it yet.

When Jesus walked the earth, He encountered all kinds of struggling people. He got to know them and shared truth through easy-to-remember parables and stories, metaphors, and turns of phrase. But eventually, He spoke plainly—as He did in John 16. He got to the heart of the matter and the lightbulb went on for the ones He loved and led. As recovery leaders, we're meant to follow this mode.

AS YOU GROW IN RELATIONSHIP WITH RECOVERING PEOPLE, KEEP ONE EAR ON THE CONVERSATION AND ONE EAR ON THE HOLY SPIRIT SO YOU KNOW WHEN TO SHIFT GEARS.

As you grow in relationship with recovering people, I urge you to follow the nudge of the Holy Spirit so you know when it's time to change the conversation. Calibrate invitational, friendly language with more challenging, vulnerable language at the appropriate times. Keep one ear on the conversation and one ear on the Holy Spirit so you know when to shift gears.

For example, if you suspect someone is struggling with suicidal thoughts, skip vague and leading inquiries such as, "Are you doing okay this week?" or "How's life treating you?" Even the marginally more direct, "You're not thinking about killing yourself, are you?" makes most people-pleasers lie and respond with an adamant, "Oh, no!" Looking them in the eye with love and compassion and asking, "Are you thinking about killing yourself?" can mean the difference between life and death. They will struggle to look you in the eye and lie, even if it's what they think you want to hear.

The same applies to people struggling with mental health problems. If you suspect someone is not taking their medication, don't beat around the bush. Direct and specific questions like, "Did you take your medication this morning?" and "Have you taken your full dosage of medication every day this week?" can uncover opportunities for intervention that could keep them from spiraling out of control or becoming a danger to themselves and others.

Addiction is no different, although accountability here can be trickier than you might think. Even with sponsorship models built into most traditional recovery programming, we struggle to stay the course in holding people accountable, especially when it seems like they're sober. Saying, "Are you high right now?" is relatively easy when you know it's true. "Did you use this week?" can feel accusatory when you can't prove it. Addiction is easy to hide… until it isn't. God loves us too much to allow us to continue to live with addiction forever. If we don't answer His call to come home, He will come after us like Francis Thompson's "The Hound of Heaven," chasing after us with His love no matter where we may run, reconciling us back to Himself at any cost.

FROM FUNCTIONAL TO FALLING APART

People struggling with addiction can go from functional to falling apart in a moment, still believing they're in full control. God uses these sobering moments to encounter us as we encounter Him. Just ask my friend Chris.

On the surface, Chris had everything going for him. He was tall, good looking, smart, charismatic, and ridiculously talented. He was drafted to play professional baseball at age eighteen, with more money, power, women, and freedom than most people would know what to do with. He fell hard under the weight of his addictions and nearly lost everything, including his life.

Despite most people's assumptions, Chris didn't grow up with everything. After his seventeen-year-old mother chose her addiction over him, he was raised by his widowed German immigrant grandmother in central Florida. Her husband had struggled with alcohol and died of cirrhosis of the liver before Chris was born. When his grandmother remarried, Chris found a solid father figure who taught him how to play baseball. Chris's loving, faithful family wasn't exactly a churchgoing one, but he went by himself to services in town. Church, like home, was a place where he felt truly loved and free to be a kid.

But beyond the safety of church and home, trauma and abuse awaited Chris. He struggled with attention deficient hyperactivity disorder and his confidence waned. To make matters much worse, he was sexually molested by multiple men for years on end. Every one of his identity lines started to blur. No longer able to tell the difference between love and abuse, he sought out his molesters for attention until he eventually became one himself, watching porn with and performing graphic sexual acts on his peers as a normalized activity.

Despite the insecurity in his sex life, Chris came into his own in high school through baseball. He was naturally gifted and universally loved by family, friends, and fans. It was during this season of life that he first questioned the sexual abuse from his past. Once he experienced love in the *right* way, it brought the many *wrong* ways he had experienced it into the light. Chris grew in confidence and embraced a bigger purpose in his sport, but he remained bound in an addictive mindset and used his star-athlete status to not just play the field but dominate it. After his first-love high school girlfriend broke up with him, Chris's mental health spiraled into full-on sexual addiction, which resulted in continued confusion and countless disposable relationships.

Shortly after graduation, Chris got his big break. He was drafted by the Chicago Cubs. He signed a contract, played his first season in the Windy City, and came home during the off-season with plenty of money, fame, and talent—but no work ethic whatsoever. He spent the majority of his time off completely stoned, doing just about anything for sex. He sobered up for spring training the following year, but broke his left pinky toe and was sent back home for the season to heal. In his depression and boredom, he spiraled even deeper. Marijuana and alcohol gave way to cocaine, acid, and eventually crack. Despite this roller coaster, he managed to play professional baseball for five more years before the Cubs released him, and Chris went from full-time baseball to full-time partying. His career in ruins, Chris couldn't shake the thought that he'd disappointed everyone he loved. His grandmother, step-grandfather, and mother all died in a swift season of loss. Chris was crippled with devastating depression. That's when he met Lisa.

She was a sweet, salt-of-the-earth Sicilian with a broken past and a shattered spirit. She, too, had just lost her mother, so Chris and Lisa were bound together in their grief. Through a string of compounding lies, Chris managed to win over Lisa and marry her; he was convinced that settling down, getting a job, and starting a family would keep him sober. It didn't. When Chris and Lisa's son Nicholas came along in 2007, Chris was thrilled, but Lisa was terrified. By their son's first birthday, Chris's addiction was wildly out of control. When Lisa finally kicked him out of their townhouse, his downward spiral continued for two years until Chris sold a girlfriend's car and spent $9,000 on a three-day crack bender that nearly killed him. It was on the heels of this near-death experience that our mutual friend Charles gave Chris my number—and Chris was introduced to the Timothy Initiative.

"When you want recovery, you chase it," Chris recalls. And man, did Chris chase it. After nearly losing his life to addiction, he was all in, eager to be part of our T.I. community. He loved living on-site because he was never alone. He loved Bible study and church because he knew he was accepted. He even loved doing construction work with Initiative Builds—until he got what he thought was the better offer he had been praying for: a fantastic, high-paying job as a mortgage broker.

Chris was convinced this new gig would help him put his life and family back together. I was skeptical, but very eager to encourage Chris, so I agreed to let him take the job and work off-site—as long as he allowed me to help manage his finances and spent his time off back in community with us. It went well for several months. Until one day, instead of going home after work, Chris went to a bar, bought some crack, and relapsed. He didn't understand why or how it had happened. I realized then that Chris wasn't yet ready for the full responsibilities of a promised-land life, and I hadn't been direct enough in my accountability conversations.

So with the Holy Spirit's leading, I shifted from invitation to challenge. I told Chris that after an intensive, six-month detoxification program, he would be welcome to come back to stay in community with us on one condition—he had to quit the job. Chris refused, convinced he already had the tools he needed to manage his addiction on his own. One evening while he was packing and preparing to leave us, our men's Bible study prayed over Chris and a miracle happened. We didn't change his mind—but the Holy Spirit got ahold of Chris and transformed his heart and mind. The next day, he quit his job and started the six-month detox. And six months later, he came back home to T.I.

Chris's progress was so astounding, even his wife took notice. Lisa began allowing Chris to see his son on a regular basis and began to actively support and encourage him in his recovery. Chris still secretly clung to the idea of a family restored, even after Lisa filed paperwork for divorce. Although Lisa still cared for Chris and wanted him in her son's life, she finally confessed that she had been seeing someone else and had no plans to reconcile. Chris was shattered but didn't turn to his old vices. Instead, he surrendered his wife and son to God and promised to be the best father and ex-husband he could possibly be.

> A FUNNY THING HAPPENS WHEN WE LET GO OF CONTROL. LIFE DOESN'T ALWAYS GET BETTER RIGHT AWAY, BUT THE WAY WE SEE OUR LIVES STARTS TO GET BETTER.

A funny thing happens when we let go of control. Life doesn't always get better right away, but the way we see our lives starts to get better. Chris was thriving in the T.I. Recovery house. In time, he was ready and able to get another job in finance and start saving and planning for his future. In this fruitful transition season, Chris made good on his promise to God, stepping up and making time for Lisa and Nicholas at every turn. He continually asked her, "How can I help make your life easier? What can I do?" His love and devotion was evident to her, even with no hope or expectation of reconciliation. *But God.* A year later, Chris began dating his wife. It wasn't long before she dropped the divorce papers, and they asked me to renew their vows.

Today, Chris is reunited with his family, working as a successful mortgage broker, and volunteering in recovery ministries throughout central Florida. Their family is still a core part of our T.I. family—Nicholas, now a teenager, learned to swim in our pool and still lovingly calls T.I. leaders like me, Joe, and Mike "the guys." Chris's miraculous Spirit-led journey was only made possible by breaking down and rebuilding a life that looked great on the surface but needed an influx of healing, hope, and, yes—a little tough love. This is the kind of promised-land life that can only come by way of the Uncovery.

PAST PAIN, FUTURE GAIN

We already know that eight out of ten of people in recovery from addiction, mental health problems, and suicidal thoughts won't make it to one year without a relapse. This is because the early stages of recovery are focused so heavily on self-centered behavior modification strategies. People want the car, the job, the family—good things that may in fact be a part of a promised-land life. But when people win big before transformation occurs, the short-term goals that drive them aren't enough to keep them sober and free from the underlying issue that led to their trouble in the first place.

Those who do make it to year one without relapse are likely to experience it before years two and three are over. The first three years of recovery are hands down the most challenging, but they're also the most foundational. Those who make it to three years will be the ones who experience decades of freedom because they have developed the ability to look beyond their own self-centered goals to more intrinsic, Christ-centered ones. The Uncovery allows room for the time it takes to grow in spiritual maturity. It's more than a flip-switch moment of enlightenment; it's a disciplined willingness to make daily decisions that lead to a promised-land life.

Recovery *is* life—and here's why.

I don't check many doctrinal or denominational boxes, but my theology is quite simple: God is far more than a *higher power*. He is no less than *good Father* to me. And I make it my mission to let everyone I encounter know how much He really loves and forgives them.

I don't care who you are, where you're from, or what you've done—you deserve to know the truth. *God is absolutely in love with you.* Right now. And He wants you to come home to Him, just as you are, and let His perfect love transform your heart and mind forever.

What could possibly keep us from this incredible offer of unconditional love and full-on adoption, with no strings attached? How could anyone ever say no? Because deep, *deep* down, the lies we believe can get really, *really* loud. Lies from the enemy, lies we tell ourselves, and even lies people speak over us directly. They might sound something like this:

+ You're just an addict/mental case/coward/sinner, and you always will be.

+ How could God ever love you after what you've done?

+ You're not worthy of love from God—or from anyone, for that matter.

+ Your sins are unforgiveable and so are you.

+ You'd better clean up your act if you want God to forgive you.

+ You're damaged goods; why would God want you?

+ There's no grace left for you—you've used your share.

+ You may be healed, but your scars are still showing.

+ God is so disappointed in you that you embarrass Him.

+ You may be saved, but you'll do something to screw it up.

+ The world would be better off without you in it.

No matter who is telling us these hideous lies, they keep us from believing God could possibly love us the way He does. When our identities stay stuck in who we *think* we are, where we're from, and what we've done, for better or worse, we can't possibly embrace our true identities as beloved children of God.

This kingdom identity isn't a family of origin, but one you get to be reborn into. It's not a region you hail from, but a place of truth you get to discover and claim as your own. It has nothing to do with your accomplishments or failures and everything to do with the goodness and grace of God. It's not about you. It's about *Him.*

> WHEN OUR IDENTITIES STAY STUCK IN WHO WE THINK WE ARE, WHERE WE'RE FROM, AND WHAT WE'VE DONE, WE CAN'T POSSIBLY EMBRACE OUR TRUE IDENTITIES AS BELOVED CHILDREN OF GOD.

The pain of the past can be real and lasting. And while much of the church and much of the world would encourage traumatized people to just "get past it," the Uncovery provides another way forward. The justification we get by our faith rewrites our past in a way that allows us to stand innocent before a holy God, fully known and fully loved. The Father forgives and forgets our sins— He's just awesome like that. But He doesn't forget our past—He redeems it.

> *Praise the LORD, my soul, and forget not all his benefits— who **forgives all your sins** and **heals all your diseases**, who **redeems your life from the pit** and **crowns you with love and compassion.*** (Psalm 103:2–4)

If we're willing, I believe God pays back what's been stolen from us through our pain and trauma *sevenfold* (see Proverbs 6:31) when we allow Him to rewrite our stories from the viewpoint of heaven.

I don't believe God is the originator of our pain. It's not in His character as a good Father to cause us harm, especially after what Jesus did on the cross. But for the painful things God allows in our lives that I still struggle to accept, it helps to remember this purpose-led truth: We go through what we go through to help others go through what we went through. The apostle Paul explains it best in his second letter to the early church in Corinth.

> *Praise be to the God and Father of our Lord Jesus Christ, the Father of compassion and the God of all comfort,* **who comforts us in all our troubles, so that we can comfort those in any trouble with the comfort we ourselves receive from God.**   (2 Corinthians 1:3–4)

We may never fully grasp the problem of pain in this world. Jesus told us plainly, *"In this world you will have trouble. But take heart! I have overcome the world"* (John 16:33). If I've learned anything from those red-letter aha moments with Father, Son, and Holy Spirit, it's this: We can take Jesus, the Word, at His word.

This is where the Uncovery comes in. On the other side of pain is joy. On the other side of trauma is healing. And on the other side of abuse is advocacy. There's no way around it, over it, or underneath it. The only way out—the *best* way out—is through. When we choose to live life on purpose, through the good, the bad, and especially the ugly, our greatest places of pain can be transformed into our greatest places of influence.

QUESTIONS FOR REFLECTION

1. How has the problem of pain impacted your life and/or recovery journey?

_____

_____

_____

_____

_____

2. How can you use more direct language when holding people accountable?

_____

_____

_____

_____

_____

3. What stood out to you about Chris's roller-coaster story of redemption?

_____

_____

_____

_____

_____

9

RECOVERY AND THE GOSPEL

*Whoever wants to save their life will lose it, but whoever
loses their life for me and for the gospel will save it.*
—Mark 8:35

In recovery circles, you don't often hear someone say, "I've arrived." Trained counselors know that when you do, it can actually be a cause for concern. This confidence can leave faithful twelve-steppers and box-checkers feeling invincible...until life inevitably gets in the way. That's because life, even a *transformed* one, can be ridiculously hard. Thankfully, even the promised-land life we work toward in the Uncovery isn't our final destination. Instead, it's part of a rebirth into the eternal life we're all being invited to experience.

Sobriety is to recovery what salvation is to Christianity. From a practical standpoint, this means that all people who call themselves Christian are in recovery. We're all trying to get healed and whole, to get back to who the Father created us to be, to realize the abundant life that Jesus went to the cross for us to have.

When we say *no* to our struggles, especially for the very first time, it can create the same clean-slate euphoria as when we first say *no* to sin and *yes* to Jesus. Even if we were forced into rehab or bullied to the altar, initial sobriety and initial salvation remain powerful and important milestones along the Uncovery journey.

However, the lie we often believe is that *getting sober* or *getting saved* will make all of life's problems go away. When they don't, it causes us to question God's character and our identity. We think:

+ *God, if You're a good Father, how could You let this happen?*

+ *God, if You love me, why does it feel like You've abandoned me?*

+ *God, why aren't You answering me? Are You even there at all?*

You wouldn't be the first person to ask these questions. At the end of the book of Deuteronomy, after initial deliverance from slavery in Egypt and wandering in the desert for forty years, the mantle of leadership over the Israelites passed from Moses to Joshua. Before he died, Moses told Joshua and the people exactly what to do when they crossed over into the promised land. Fight the giants? Set up camp? Throw a party? Nope. He told them to grab some stones.

> *Build there an altar to the* LORD *your God, an altar of stones. Do not use any iron tool on them. Build the altar of the* LORD *your God with fieldstones and offer burnt offerings on it to the* LORD *your God. Sacrifice fellowship offerings there, eating them and rejoicing in the presence of the* LORD *your God. And you shall write very clearly all the words of this law on these stones you have set up.*   (Deuteronomy 27:5–8)

As the story transitions from Deuteronomy into the book of Joshua, the Israelites have another dramatic supernatural deliverance. Forty years after their Red Sea encounter, God split the waters once again so His people could cross over the Jordan River on dry land into the promised land. When the whole nation had finished crossing—except for a handful of priests who remained in the middle path holding the ark of the covenant—Joshua heard another word about stones. Except this time, the directive wasn't coming from Moses. It was coming from God Himself.

> *Choose twelve men from among the people, one from each tribe, and tell them to take up twelve stones from the middle of the Jordan, from right where the priests are standing, and carry them over with you and put them down at the place where you stay tonight.* (Joshua 4:2–3)

Joshua did what God asked. He gathered the tribal leaders and told them to go back onto the riverbed and get the stones so that one day they could tell their children about the miracle that occurred. Once the stones were out and the priests crossed over, the waters of the Jordan came crashing back down again. The Israelites set up the stones of remembrance at Gilgal on the eastern border of Jericho as Moses had described. This was a significant moment for the Israelites, and a testament to God's faithfulness that would last for generations.

But Joshua and the Israelites were just getting started. There were still plenty of battles ahead. (Hello, Jericho.) But God knew, and the Israelites experienced, just how powerful it can be to set up reminders so we don't forget what He has done in the past.

Setting up stone memorials became commonplace for believers. The more memorial stones we have in our lives, whether literal or figurative, the better. Many Old Testament prophets followed Joshua's lead, including Samuel with his famous Ebenezer stone of help and the twelve stones on Elijah's rebuilt altar. (See 1 Samuel 7:12 and 1 Kings 18:30–32, respectively.) Memorial stones like these encouraged future generations to remember God's faithfulness to show up as a good Father, no matter what. Faith in the Father's faithfulness can mean the difference between life and death.

When I launched the Sober Truth Project in 2020, many people questioned our three-tier recovery approach. The focus on addiction and mental health problems as distinct struggles made sense to most people, but an entire category dedicated to suicide prevention raised a lot of questions. They asked, "Aren't suicidal thoughts just a mental health problem? Isn't that splitting hairs?" Well, yes—and no. Suicidal thoughts may be related to a mental health problem. They may also be linked to an addiction, just as addiction and mental health problems often go hand in hand. We like to categorize our issues into neat, tidy little boxes instead of exploring the interconnectedness of the human condition. But I digress.

> SUICIDAL THOUGHTS MAY BE RELATED TO A MENTAL HEALTH PROBLEM OR AN ADDICTION. THE ISSUE DOESN'T FIT INTO A NEAT, TIDY LITTLE BOX.

I have three important reasons for calling out suicidal thoughts into its own category:

1. Suicide is often the result of unresolved addiction and mental health problems.

2. Loved ones rarely know how to help—or how to cope after a suicide.

3. We're not talking about suicide enough, especially in Christian recovery.

If we know lives and souls are at stake when it comes to suicide, why aren't we, the church, talking—and doing—something about it? Two words: bad theology.

Early Christian church fathers, including Augustine and Aquinas, rightfully saw suicide as a "killing of the innocent."[25] But

25. Robert Barry, "The Development of the Roman Catholic Teachings on Suicide," *Notre Dame Journal of Law, Ethics & Public Policy*, 449 (1995), scholarship.law.nd.edu/ndjlepp/vol9/iss2/4.

their applied teachings implied that committing suicide would send a person straight to hell for murder, pointing to people like Judas Iscariot for biblical backup.

THE STIGMA OF SUICIDE

Although the modern church's views on suicide have softened dramatically in light of increased mental health awareness, the stigmas that follow generations of shame, bullying, and bad teaching around suicide still prevail in the church. Some *name it and claim it* denominations even forbid people to say the word *suicide* out loud for fear it will manifest within the congregation.

Deep down, we know refusing to name and deal with our struggles doesn't solve anything. And yet here we are, shushing and shaming struggling people instead of setting them free in Jesus's name.

I speak with authority on this subject, not only as someone who is privileged to minister to people who struggle with suicidal thoughts and ideation on a daily basis, but as someone who has lived it. Between the ages of sixteen and thirty-five, I attempted suicide six times. The doctors labeled it "persistent suicidal ideation." My complex identity struggles were dramatically escalated through drug and alcohol abuse, and I was a dead man walking for most of my life. Each suicide attempt was met not with compassion, but contempt. My first intentional overdose on pills at age sixteen resulted in an emergency room doctor's empty threat to press charges against me for attempted murder. The condemning phrases of downstream attempts still haunt me:

+ What have you done?

+ You are so selfish.

+ How could you?

+ You just want attention.

＋ Who do you think you are?

My attempts were eventually met with legal action when the Florida Mental Health Act of 1971, widely known as the "Baker Acts," allowed the state to institutionalize me against my will for observation and examination by order of a judge, police officer, physician, or mental health professional.

Did any these shaming, forceful, matter-of-fact responses help me? In some ways, maybe—in other ways, not so much. But I learned firsthand that God's hand was in it all. We go through what we go through to help others go through what we went through. And as with most struggles we face in this life, the only way out for me was through.

Unfortunately, many religious communities respond to suicidal thoughts and ideation with as much compassion as medical and legal communities do—which is to say, not so much. When I minister to people struggling with suicidal thoughts and ideation, after each episode, I make sure to directly ask why they chose not to take their own life. The answer is almost always, "I'm afraid I'll go to hell." That old, bad theology keeps struggling people held in a false, legalistic limbo when they truly need to hear the truth about the gospel and the hope that comes with it.

Fear of hell can be a strong motivator to keep people from sin, but fear of hell and fear of God are two *very* different things. The first will affirm the sinner identity, while the second will reveal the saint identity.

SUICIDAL THOUGHTS OCCUR WHEN PEOPLE DON'T BELIEVE THEY'RE LOVED OR FORGIVEN AND DON'T BELIEVE THERE IS HOPE AND AN ABUNDANT LIFE WAITING FOR THEM.

Suicidal thoughts are part of an identity disorder. It occurs when people don't believe they're loved, don't believe they're forgiven, and don't believe there is hope and an abundant life waiting for them. We, the church, need to accept responsibility for it and lead people from death to life. This is the power of the Uncovery and the gospel.

FAIR WARNING

Accepting responsibility to love and lead people struggling with suicidal thoughts will break your heart. Once you see suicide for what it is—the absence of hope—you begin to see it everywhere. What you focus on expands, not because you're manifesting it, but because so many people are struggling with suicidal thoughts in silence. As recovery leaders, God gives us eyes to see and opportunities to go deeper than we have before. About a decade after my brother and sister died after seemingly accidental overdoses, another pair of senseless deaths hit our community and shook me to the core.

For many years, I wore locks in my hair. It was a bold look for a white guy, I know, but I was willing to put in the three hours it took every couple of months to keep my inner and outer wild child going strong. This gave me an abundance of quality time with Alyssa, my hairdresser. I don't know what it is about that spinning salon chair that makes people open up to stylists, but Alyssa felt like a safe friend to be vulnerable and real with from day one.

On the outside, Alyssa had everything going for her. She was strong, smart, and strikingly beautiful. She wasn't a Christian, but she was highly spiritual and seeking, so we had plenty to discuss. We talked about everything as she twisted each lock—faith and family, music and tattoos, and, of course, our own recovery journeys. She was tough, but I'd catch a little crack in her armor now and then. She'd ask me an impossibly deep spiritual question or share a shocking piece of unfolding trauma from her own story. But I always thought, *If anyone can make it through this life, it's Alyssa.*

Hurt people don't just hurt other people. They hurt themselves, too. Alyssa's brother-in-law, my tattoo artist, called me with the news early on a Thursday morning. Alyssa had died by suicide. After all of those hours we spent talking while she did my hair and more than a decade in recovery ministry, I still didn't see it coming.

On the Saturday morning after Alyssa's death, while I was trying to find the words to say to her family for the upcoming memorial service, I got a phone call from Kevin, one of our Timothy Initiative board members. (You may remember Kevin and his wife Kathleen from chapter four; they are the ones who so graciously forgave Bo for putting their car through its paces.) Our donor relationship had grown into a deep and authentic friendship over the years, and I assumed Kevin was calling to comfort me because of Alyssa's death. But when I answered, the tremble in Kevin's usually rock-steady voice suggested something entirely different.

Now, Kevin and Kathleen had always inspired me. They were global kingdom entrepreneurs with a *business as mission* mindset that brought much-needed sustainability to the Timothy Initiative's ministry model with Initiative Builds. I'll never forget the first time they toured our early T.I. community as prospective donors. They brought their two teenagers with them, Kevin Jr. and his little sister Ashley, which made me hyperconscious of how our T.I. guys were behaving. I expected Kevin and Kathleen to grill me with the typical box-checking questions for which I would struggle to find answers. But this kingdom-focused family was full of surprises.

"Kids, what questions do you have for George about his ministry?" Kevin asked earnestly. His son, who was in seventh grade at the time, jumped at the opportunity and started peppering me with questions:

+ How many men do you think you can help?

+ How many people could live here at one time?

+ How many salvations do you think you'll see?

+ How can we help you introduce people to Jesus?

As the questions rolled in, I stood there wide-eyed and delighted. I'd never seen so much love pouring out from someone so young.

The family went all in with T.I. and Kevin Jr. was at the forefront of it all. He stayed with us. He ate with us. He worked with us. He did life with us. He grew up with our motley crew—volunteering on-site, leading worship at our Bible studies, and participating in mission trips, living and working with our Initiative Builds crew. He always came to me eager to share and hungry for more, with questions about life, love, faith, friendship, and leadership. The kid became a spiritual son to me in the truest sense and I began to love him as one of my own. He grew into a powerful emerging leader—preaching and evangelizing, leading local and global missions in China, Tibet, Thailand, South America, Ecuador, Peru, and more. He loved well, and he walked humbly. He stayed well-connected through his college years as his influence skyrocketed, and we all surrounded him and sent him on mission as a family.

Kevin Jr. was on fire for Jesus. But there's a fine line between being on fire and being on edge. Kevin Jr.'s charisma overshadowed a growing multitude of struggles—a trend we're now seeing from Christian faith leaders of all persuasions. That phone call from Kevin Sr. and Kathleen wasn't to comfort me—it was to ask *me* to comfort *them*. Kevin Jr. had jumped off the Skyway Bridge in Tampa and died by suicide. Nobody saw it coming—not even me, someone who should have seen it by definition of my calling.

Most suicides end with family members and close friends alike admitting they had no idea their loved one was struggling. And yet...when they scroll through text messages, listen to old voice mails, and see the exhaustion in their loved ones' eyes in recent photos, they may wonder if there was a moment when they should have seen a sign—and been more direct. While we can't go back and make a difference in the lives of the ones we've loved and lost, we can learn from the experiences how to better love and lead people who are struggling with suicidal thoughts and how to surround and grieve with families who suffer in the aftermath of loss.

> WHILE WE CAN'T GO BACK AND MAKE A DIFFERENCE IN THE LIVES OF THE ONES WE'VE LOVED AND LOST, WE CAN LEARN FROM THE EXPERIENCES HOW TO BETTER LOVE AND LEAD PEOPLE WHO ARE STRUGGLING.

The world keeps turning, but life without Kevin Jr. is difficult to comprehend. His story is by far the most shocking and painful one of my life. I still cry out to the Father in utter frustration, and the pain is still every bit as raw as the moment I heard the news. As Julie and I continue to do life with his parents, trying to make sense of Kevin Jr.'s death seems even more futile than trying to make sense of my siblings' deaths. The less you expect to stare death in the face, the more painful it can be.

Late the next week, I spoke with Alyssa's family in the morning before racing across town to help Kevin and Kathleen mourn the loss of Kevin Jr. The back-to-back, senseless losses of Alyssa and Kevin Jr. mirrored and triggered memories of the senseless losses of my own sister and brother. As Julie and I drove from one memorial to another, numb with disbelief, we knew our pain was rooted in our call to *talk* more and *do* more about suicide. We were called to grieve with those who mourn, but the Father was asking us to leverage that grief for our good and His glory in ways the church had never done before.

ISSUES ARE OFTEN INTERCONNECTED

One reason I was moved with compassion to write this book was to shed light on the merciless and indiscriminate nature of suicide in the hopes that even one person might choose a promised-land life over death. At one point or another, suicide will touch your life if it hasn't already. If processing painful stories of love and loss could help even one recovery leader, one family member, or one friend learn to better recognize the signs of suicidal behavior and intervene, it would be worth it—even if that person is me. Goodness knows we all have more to learn.

When I started the Timothy Initiative, I was laser-focused on helping broken men get free from addiction, particularly to drugs and alcohol. The more I learned about trauma-informed ministry, spiritual predisposition, and the interconnectedness of addiction, mental health problems, and suicidal thoughts, the more I came to realize my call was being extended to broad-ranging recovery areas. One such appointment was to Christian—a guy most people never would have expected to end up with our T.I. crew. He was nineteen when I met him, yet he had already been walking in the wilderness for what seemed like several lifetimes.

Christian's parents divorced when he was just eighteen months old, leaving him and his older brother bouncing back and forth between two very different households. His dad was an any-thing-goes free spirit, while his mom was much more straightlaced and demanding. In his youth, Christian gravitated toward his "fun" dad, and their relationship turned dysfunctional in a hurry. At age thirteen, Christian was sexually abused by his father and his father's girlfriend. Confused, hurt, and ashamed, he hid the abuse from everyone, including his mother. The pain and dissonance escalated until Christian had a huge falling out with his dad and moved out. He chose a fatherless life at age fifteen. Shortly after the argument, his father suffered a major heart attack. Christian swallowed his pride, went to the hospital with his brother, and held his father's hand as he flatlined.

This coming-of-age season of trauma and loss launched Christian into a dark season. If God was real, he wanted nothing to do with Him. And who could blame him? Christian couldn't wrap his tormented mind around what an earthly father was supposed to be, and what he learned in church as a kid about an all-powerful heavenly Father seemed somehow even more disturbing. Christian made it through high school by the skin of his teeth and enrolled in a two-year culinary arts program. He partied and slept his way through college, drinking, smoking marijuana, and chasing girls. Until he met *the* girl—the one who would send his life on a completely different trajectory.

She was perfect—beautiful, smart, talented, and even "a part-time Christian," as Christian describes it. Leaning deep into her double life, she and Christian partied and even lived together. But eventually she convinced him to meet her Jesus friends. He went in on the offensive, armed with all the tough questions he wanted God to answer. "Why did my dad have to die? Why do bad things happen to good people?" To Christian's surprise, these Jesus friends remained unfazed. They did their best to answer his questions, lovingly and free of judgment. This group felt different. It felt safe.

The more time Christian spent with the group, the more he wanted to be with them—and somehow with God by proxy. He decided to go with them on a mission trip to (you guessed it) Tampa, Florida, to do a week of construction with the Underground. He connected with me, met Timothy Initiative brothers, and admitted that this recovery group seemed less like the humdrum Christian cults he had experienced and more like the movie *Fight Club*. The authentic Christian camaraderie and friendships built on the job led to a restful encounter with God on a Sarasota beach. He gave his life to Jesus and even got baptized. But that initial deliverance was just the beginning of his journey.

Christian returned home and resumed life as usual. And then, *the* girl—the one who changed the trajectory of his life—cheated on him. Despite being saved, Christian spiraled into a deep depression and began struggling with suicidal ideation. Running on a toxic mix of marijuana, alcohol, and amphetamines, he wrote a suicide note, strapped two belts around a pull-up bar in his apartment, and leapt forward to hang himself. Everything went dark. Inexplicably, Christian woke up in a ball on the floor, sobbing, gasping for air, and thinking, *God, please—kill me or give me something different.*

A friend from the group of Jesus people checked in on Christian, knowing he was struggling. He invited him to go back to Tampa for another mission trip with the Underground to clear his head, reminding him how welcomed and loved he felt there. Christian finally gave in. Florida felt different—and safe. He not only came back to Tampa, he stayed here with us at the Timothy Initiative for six years!

He wasn't our typical community member; he never did hardcore drugs or got into trouble with the law. But we unpacked and dealt with his trauma and unique struggles on God's timing. Christian recovered, healed, and stepped into a promised-land life worth living by walking out his unique Uncovery journey. He's ministered around the world and introduced so many people to Christ—and he's only twenty-five years old! Today he lives independently, works as a contractor, and continues to minister to broken men on the job, sharing the good news of hope he's found in a good Father God. I am so proud of him and I can't wait to watch him do greater things than I ever could for the kingdom. I thank God every day that He delivered Christian from death to life by the power of the Holy Spirit. I want to see more people walking out resurrection lives like Christian, in eager anticipation of what's next. His story is proof positive that not even a suicide attempt can disqualify you from the Father's call on your life.

WALKING IT OUT

There will be fierce battles during the Uncovery, even on the far side of the Jordan in the promised land, when we think we should be home free. This is where we can be tempted to lose hope. It was true for the Israelites, and it's true for us today. Some setbacks and obstacles will build character and strengthen our spiritual resolve. Some will steal our breath, leaving us with no option other than to go back to the Father for the comfort only He can provide.

In these moments, we realize that it's in Him that *"we live and move and have our being"* (Acts 17:28). We can't even have faith on our own. We need Him. And when He allows trauma, suffering, and loss in our lives, we can trust that He's allowing it to draw us closer to Him and bring us into an even deeper place of recovery, healing, and oneness than we could ever imagine.

The hard heart work of recovery typically reveals one of two things about us:

1. Our natural tendency toward *brokenness* (original sin), or

2. Our natural tendency toward *righteousness* (original blessing)

WHETHER WE CONCLUDE THAT WE'RE BROKEN OR RIGHTEOUS IS GREATLY INFLUENCED BY THE PEOPLE SURROUNDING US AND THE TYPES OF SPIRITUAL BATTLES WE CHOOSE TO FIGHT TOGETHER.

The conclusion we come to—"I'm broken" or "I'm righteous"—is greatly influenced by the people we choose to surround ourselves with and the types of spiritual battles we choose to fight together. For better or worse, the conclusion we come to contains a confirmation bias that will shape our identities and frame up the way we live out the rest of our days in this world and in the next.

+ If we believe we're broken, and we always will be? *We'll walk it out.* And stay broken.

+ If we believe we're nothing more than sinners saved by grace? *We'll walk it out.* And keep on sinning.

+ On the other hand, if we believe we've been made righteous through Jesus? *We'll walk it out.* And let go of shame.

+ And if we believe that nothing can separate us from the Father's love? *We'll walk it out.* And embrace our true identities.

I know we're dipping our toes into some controversial theological waters here, so let me be clear: I'm not calling anyone's salvation into question here. That's way above my pay grade. But friends, I believe we're being invited to go beyond initial sobriety—and initial salvation—to embrace a promised-land life with confidence, certain of our identity as beloved sons and daughters of a good Father.

There is an abundant life waiting for each and every one of us that's 100 percent worth living. Setbacks and obstacles will come—Jesus Himself told us so—but the hope we carry paves the way for the joy that's set before us. (See Hebrews 12:1–3.) We can overcome anything we face because Jesus overcame sin and death when He willingly sacrificed Himself for us nearly two thousand years ago.

Jesus didn't die by suicide. But His willingness to die for us and for our sins created the abundant, eternal life to which we all have access. Sin and death were defeated by Jesus's death and resurrection. When Jesus died, you died with Him. And when He came back to life, so did you. Death—and even suicidal thoughts—have no authority over you anymore.

The gospel is actually quite simple: Jesus died so you didn't have to. That wild gift of grace gives us hope for a promised-land life that's worth staying sober for. Receiving and releasing this gift over struggling people is the most powerful tool we, the church, have against death by suicide. It's up to us to make sure the world understands the grace they've been freely given, even the ones who seem to have it all together—especially them. May we never again have to utter the words, "I never saw it coming."

Recovery isn't just *like* the gospel. It *is* the gospel. And if suicide is the absence of hope, the gospel is the presence of hope in the person of Jesus. His death and resurrection applied within the framework of the Uncovery are humankind's greatest hope. I've seen recurring evidence that receiving and embracing the Father's gift of grace fully—as the core of our identity—cancels out spirits of suicide and death. Once you encounter the Father's love, you realize there is always *Someone* who longs to share a promised-land life with you.

When we believe *Hope Himself* is within our reach? *We'll walk it out*. And move from death to life by the power of the Holy Spirit.

QUESTIONS FOR REFLECTION

1. What ties do you see between recovery and salvation?

---

2. Have you spent any time researching methods of suicide prevention? If so, what have you learned? If not, why not?

---

3. Who do you know right now who might be at risk for suicide? What first step might you take to open a dialogue with them?

10

RECOVERY AND REVIVAL

*Have I not commanded you? **Be strong and courageous.***
Do not be afraid; do not be discouraged, for the LORD your
God will be with you wherever you go.
—Joshua 1:9

"**B**e *strong and courageous.*" Of the twenty-five times God says these four empowering words in Scripture, four of them are directed at Joshua—once before he led the Israelites over the Jordan riverbed into the promised land (Deuteronomy 31:23), and three times afterward (Joshua 1:6, 7, 9). God not only knew He would need to offer continual encouragement and reinforcement for the battles ahead in the promised land, He knew Joshua and his people needed a deeper understanding of who *He* was as Father and who *they* were in Him on their collective identity journey.

This continual, pressed-in emphasis on identity—not only as individuals but corporately—is the foundational basis for the Uncovery. It's fascinating to realize that identity is also the foundational basis for the spiritual revival we all want to see in the Christian church today, about 3,500 years after the Israelites' initial deliverance from captivity.

God's directive to Joshua to embody strength and courage was not meant to shame him. The Father doesn't tell people to pull themselves up by their bootstraps and neither should we. Each time the Father commands these virtues, He offers an invitation to tap into His own strength and courage—strength that is made perfect in our weakness and courage that transcends human logic. This certainly didn't relieve the Israelites of their duties in preparation for battle, but it did remind them that their hope for a promised-land life was coming from a God who promised to go before them.

> *The men of Reuben, Gad and the half-tribe of Manasseh crossed over* [the Jordan River], *ready for battle, in front of the Israelites, as Moses had directed them. About forty thousand armed for battle crossed over before the* LORD *to the plains of Jericho for war.*   (Joshua 4:12–13)

God's people knew there would not only be battles *for* the promised land, but also an all-out war once they got there. At Joshua's order, they armored up in confidence, strong and courageous in the Father's strength and courage. They consecrated themselves (see Joshua 3:5) and were even circumcised (see Joshua 5:2–8) to commit their hearts, minds, and bodies to whatever God had in store for them. Even with the assurance of a promised land and every God-ordered box checked, deep down in their hearts, they knew there would be difficult days ahead. And they were right.

Are you catching the magnitude of this? The Israelites, God's chosen people, knew that *even in the promised land, there would still be battles.* So why do we, the church, assume—and in some cases even *teach*—that if we can just get people to "come to Jesus" or "get and stay sober" that their battling days will be over and done? Moreover, why do we assume our responsibility to love and lead others ends in the initial stages of salvation and sobriety?

We're living not only on the far side of the Jordan, but the far side of the cross. Why would we assume any one of us could or should have it any easier than Jesus Himself did? We might say we're willing to pick up our cross, endure persecution, and even die for the sake of the gospel, but do we really mean it?

> WHY DO WE, THE CHURCH, ASSUME THAT IF WE CAN JUST GET PEOPLE TO "COME TO JESUS" OR "GET AND STAY SOBER" THAT THEIR BATTLING DAYS WILL BE OVER AND DONE?

This might be the greatest challenge I face in loving and leading people struggling with addiction, mental health problems, and suicidal thoughts. When the going gets tough, the spiritually tough get going. But for the sober who aren't yet free and the saved who aren't yet transformed, the battles ahead aren't just daunting—they're debilitating. Even deadly. This is where we, the church, are called to bear our burdens together—not in isolation—confessing our sins to each other and praying for each other so that we may all be healed. (See James 5:16.)

This coming together of minds, hearts, and even bodies is a difficult concept to grasp in a post-pandemic world. Yes, I'm talking about COVID-19. We're going to go there. Saddle up.

Humans in general are resilient—and slowly but surely, many of us are coming out the other side of the pandemic stronger, smarter, and more sensitive to the needs of society. But what about those who didn't make it to the other side? I'm not just talking about people who lost their lives to the coronavirus or complications from the vaccines. I'm talking about people who lost their lives because of the societal impact of the lockdowns, closures, and mandates.

OVERDOSE DEATHS SKYROCKETED

The isolation we all faced sent addiction and relapses, mental health problems, and suicidal thoughts through the roof. More than 100,000 people in the United States died of drug overdoses between May 2020 and April 2021—a 28.5 percent increase from the same period in 2019–2020.[26] The monthly toll spiked to an unheard-of 9,362 overdose-related deaths in May 2020[27] when most of the known world was on lockdown. The scariest part about these numbers—and the part that will be hardest to prove by preliminary facts and data—is that *any number* of these deaths by overdose could have been intentional. Suicide rates didn't spike[28] as many of us had feared, but I believe these unprecedented levels of death by overdose may have actually been misclassified suicides.

Why aren't we studying the commonalities of death by suicide and death by accidental overdose? Some say it can't be done. I say it *must* be done. And we, the church, desperately need the scientific community's help with this so we can help people struggling with addiction and mental health problems to avoid an addict's easy-out on life itself.

Bottom line? Isolation is a killer. Events and circumstances can become trauma when we don't have people to share them with. That trauma is embedded into our memory banks as either explicit (conscious) or implicit (unconscious), and both can impact our

---

26. "Drug Overdose Deaths in the U.S. Top 100,000 Annually," Centers for Disease Control and Prevention, November 17, 2021, www.cdc.gov/nchs/pressroom/nchs_press_releases/2021/20211117.htm.
27. Jesse C. Baumgartner and David C. Radley, "The Spike in Drug Overdose Deaths During the COVID-19 Pandemic and Policy Options to Move Forward," The Commonwealth Fund, March 25, 2021, www.commonwealthfund.org/blog/2021/spike-drug-overdose-deaths-during-covid-19-pandemic-and-policy-options-move-forward.
28. Louis Appleby, "What has been the effect of covid-19 on suicide rates?" *British Medical Journal*, March 29, 2021, www.bmj.com/content/372/bmj.n834/rapid-responses.

actions and awareness. Sharing stories of trauma with a trusted member of a safe community and having those stories received with compassion can change how they impact people moving forward. If we really want to see revival, we have to figure out how to come back together again in a post-pandemic world—physically, mentally, emotionally, and spiritually—and lean on one another again. We were never meant to operate in isolation.

By now you know I don't like labels, but for simplicity's sake, I'll admit I'm actively involved in what's known as Christian revival culture. The word *revival* stirs up all kinds of emotional connotations for people, some good and some bad. At some level, revival is something we all want to see. But instead of embodying revival, we rely on our trusty systems and programs that make revival a weeklong event to schedule, complete with a marketing campaign, or another mountaintop moment to strive toward in our own strength. Revival has become something we think we can bring into its fullness without the Father participating in the process at all.

Instead of being the ones to usher in revival, we think we're the ones leading it—or worse, that we somehow *are* it. The worst part is that people trying to lead corporate revival haven't even experienced personal revival. Father, have mercy on us! Even with the best of intentions, we have no idea what we're doing.

But imagine this: What if the revival we all want to see could be attained through the Uncovery? What if it led to multitudes coming to Jesus with a renewed excitement about the gospel and our restored relationship with the Father? What if those thousands—even millions—of people who are about to step into the fullness of their identity as the Father's beloved children are the very ones who are now struggling with addiction, mental health problems, and suicidal thoughts?

If I didn't wholeheartedly believe recovery was the answer, I wouldn't be living the radical lifestyle I'm living, chasing after the same lost sheep whom Jesus seeks. Aligned with the same God Francis Thompson called "The Hound of Heaven," I will never relent in my pursuit of these precious ones who are one encounter away from stepping into an abundant, promised-land life. This pursuit takes courage, strength, and sacrifice. In some cases, it may take all you have to give.

> PURSUING GOD'S PRECIOUS LOST SHEEP TO BRING THEM TO JESUS TAKES COURAGE, STRENGTH, AND SACRIFICE.

MAYBE ALL YOU NEED IS A SANDWICH

Chasing down lost sheep isn't easy. But sometimes, it's as simple as making a sandwich.

That was the case for Lionel, a dear friend of our family. Lionel struggled with addiction and schizoaffective disorder, making it difficult for him to communicate, make eye contact, and associate people, names, or places. Most of the world saw him as a big, black, scary homeless dude with the mentality of an eight-year-old. He was often preyed upon and brutally beaten by drug pushers in our community. Julie and I always warmly welcomed Lionel at family gatherings, and he even stumbled into a Bible study or two. But he remained physically and emotionally disconnected.

A handful of our friends were wary of Lionel's presence, questioning whether Julie and I should have him around our community and especially around our kids. And to be fair, Lionel was very unpredictable. We found out just how unpredictable late one Sunday night, when I heard a frantic pounding at my front door. It was Lionel. Not knowing whether he was high, lost, confused, or in need of some serious sanctuary or intervention, I opened the door cautiously.

Lionel did something he had never done before. He looked me straight in the eye and confidently asked, "Hey! Can I get a sandwich?" I shut the door partway and turned to Julie, who was working late at the dining room table. "It's Lionel," I said. "And he wants a freaking sandwich." My irritation was less than subtle. My saintly wife looked right at me and confidently asked, "Well, are you going to make him a sandwich?" I came to my senses as I put meat and cheese between two slices of bread in the kitchen. I felt the hand of God moving me as I handed the sandwich to Lionel. Then he said, "Can I get a soda?"

Lionel took his sandwich and soda and left abruptly, without as much as a thank-you. Anyone else doing this would have been on my last nerve. Pounding on my door at all hours for food? No please or thank-you? Are you kidding me? But this was Lionel— and the whole encounter was absolutely *miraculous*!

Because he had looked at me. He knew me. He trusted me. He saw the Jesus in me and knew it was safe for him to ask for something as simple as a sandwich.

A few days later, it happened again. While driving down a divided highway around midday, I saw Lionel stumbling on the median wearing nothing but his boxer shorts. It was not his best day, for sure. I didn't know what to do. Lionel was a huge guy and when he was hallucinating, it could be dangerous to approach him alone. So I pulled up beside him and rolled down the window. He looked straight at me and said, "George! Bible study on Sunday night?" *Miraculous!* Lionel snapped out of a schizophrenic episode to interact with me, someone he knew, trusted, and saw as safe. I can't imagine what people in traffic must've thought, but I sat in awe of God's determination to connect us.

Two weeks later, Lionel passed away. Heartbroken, I cried out to the Lord. "He died! No one even cared!" And the Lord gently replied, "You cared." We were the only family Lionel had.

He mattered to us. I'll be forever thankful for the miraculous moments of connection we shared.

ARE YOU WILLING?

Are you called to love and lead people through recovery by going deeper into the Uncovery when God asks?

Are you willing to be a fellow traveler on a journey into unknown territory?

Are you willing to go on a grand adventure with no maps or GPS but a Holy Spirit compass to guide you?

> ARE YOU WILLING TO GO ON A GRAND ADVENTURE WITH NO MAPS OR GPS BUT A HOLY SPIRIT COMPASS TO GUIDE YOU?

Are you willing to lay down your reputation, your creature comforts, your religious assumptions, and even your own life for your brother or sister?

Are you willing to go the distance—to love, lead, and even *lose* people—if it might help bring recovery-led revival to a world the Father so desperately loves?

Are you willing to make a sandwich? Are you even willing to open the door?

Are you willing to ask the life-changing question, "Father, what more would You have me do?"

Jesus was willing. He made His position clear to a faith-filled leper who knelt before Him and said, *"Lord, if you are willing, you can make me clean"* (Matthew 8:2).

> *Jesus reached out his hand and touched the man. "I am willing," he said. "Be clean!" Immediately he was cleansed of his leprosy.* (Verse 3)

Whatever deep identity work you do—traditional recovery programming, counseling, inner healing, deliverance, family of origin studies, rehab centers, prayer meetings, sober-living communities, and more—keep on doing it. Please. Don't hear the message of the Uncovery and think you need to abandon ship! Your spheres of influence need you. All the Uncovery asks is that *you* continually ask, "Father, what more would You have me do?" And when He gives you something new to try, do it—without strings, hesitation, withholding, or excuses. Embrace what God has called you to do.

FIGHTING THE RIGHT BATTLES

The concept of revival brings the promised-land life full circle. And the sad reality is, some don't even choose to enter in, let alone learn to walk it out. The tribes of Reuben, Gad, and the half-tribe of Manasseh would much rather have stayed on the east side of the Jordan, never crossing the river at all.

> They came up to [Moses] and said, "We would like to build pens here for our livestock and cities for our women and children. But we will arm ourselves for battle and go ahead of the Israelites until we have brought them to their place."
> (Numbers 32:16–17)

These tribes kept their promise and helped their brothers in the conquest of Canaan. (See Joshua 22:1–4.) But they chose to settle outside the promised land. God blessed them anyway, but like so many of us, they settled for initial salvation over transformation, mere sobriety over a promised-land life. They could have done more to claim their collective inheritance, but they didn't. And the Father's grace covered them anyway.

The same is true for the refining, reforming revelation God is offering us today through His Word and through our collective experiences. No matter how hard we try, we can't make people go deeper. Sometimes people settle—and sometimes, that's okay.

If you're called to lead an AA program on Thursday evenings at your church and nothing more? Great. Lead it with everything you have. I bless you.

If you're called to love and lead one person through their recovery journey and no one else? Great. Lead them with everything you have. I bless you.

But if you know you are being called to something more...to something that scares you...to something the world would call reckless, but you know it's from God? Then listen to your good Father:

> *Have I not commanded you? Be strong and courageous. Do not be afraid; do not be discouraged, for the LORD your God will be with you wherever you go.* (Joshua 1:9)

> *The LORD himself goes before you and will be with you; he will never leave you nor forsake you. Do not be afraid; do not be discouraged.* (Deuteronomy 31:8)

> *I am the light of the world. Whoever follows me will never walk in darkness, but will have the light of life.* (John 8:12)

> *All of God's promises have been fulfilled in Christ with a resounding "Yes!"* (2 Corinthians 1:20 NLT)

Do you see it now? You *can* help hurting people because you are not alone. God is with you. All He needs is your unbridled yes.

There's no mistaking it. God has promised us a promised-land life of freedom, abundance, and intimacy with Him. Whatever side of the Jordan we're on, we must continually ask ourselves if the battles we're consecrating ourselves for are actually the battles God has called us to. When you're fighting a battle that's not for the promised land, you'll have a hard time reaching it, let alone mustering the courage to cross over into it.

> WHEN YOU'RE FIGHTING A BATTLE THAT'S NOT FOR THE PROMISED LAND, YOU'LL HAVE A HARD TIME REACHING IT, LET ALONE MUSTERING THE COURAGE TO CROSS OVER INTO IT.

Aim low and you may hit your target, but with zero transformative satisfaction. Aim high and you might not hit your target or build a perfect life, but you might shoot for the moon and land on a beautiful star—a place that feels more like home than the moon would anyway.

Ask any of my T.I. guys if they ever imagined they'd be doing life in a sober-living community that looks and acts more like a commune than most people would be comfortable with, and every single one of them would say, "No way!" Just like they never imagined they'd fall into addiction, mental health problems, or suicidal thoughts, they never saw themselves giving everything they have for the sake of the gospel and for the sake of their brothers. This promised-land life we lead is chock-full of battles for the mind, heart, body, spirit, soul, and will. When one of us struggles, we all struggle. But when one of us has victory, we share in the victory together. We're willing to look like absolute fools to the world in order to answer God's radical call on our lives. And we wouldn't be the first ones.

When Joshua marched around the walls of Jericho seven times and let out a righteous shout with his army, he looked like a fool. (See Joshua 6:15–20.) Here he was, about to head into the biggest battle he and the Israelites had faced in the promised land so far, in a manner that made zero worldly sense. If I had been Joshua (and thank God I wasn't), I'd have been more interested in picking less embarrassing fights—or at least fighting the Lord's battles in a way that didn't look so insane to everyone watching.

When Paul wrote, "*Rejoice in the Lord always. I will say it again: Rejoice!*" (Philippians 4:4) to the church in Philippi from a jail cell in Rome while awaiting possible execution, he sounded like a fool. Seriously, who does that? Who sends a letter of hope from a place with no hope? But the joy that had consumed Paul because of the good news of the gospel transcended his bondage and sparked widespread early-church revival from the most unexpected of places.

When our innocent Savior Jesus hung on a cross, dying for us and for the people who were killing Him, and He said, "*Father, forgive them, for they do not know what they are doing*" (Luke 23:34), He sounded like a fool. This level of grace was so ridiculous, onlookers laughed and sneered and scorned. They hated Him for His love for them, but He loved them all the same. Yep, even Jesus looked like a fool—but I wouldn't have wanted to be one of the executioners when the sun stopped shining and the curtain of the temple was torn in two. (See Luke 23:45.) Imagine how foolish *they* must've felt.

When you give God your yes and embrace the Uncovery, guess what? At some point, you're going to look like a fool, too. You'll stay by an addict's side far longer than people think you should. You'll compromise a boundary when God asks you to, even if it puts you or your family at risk. You'll go places you never thought you'd go, stay where you never thought you'd stay, and move in ways you never thought you'd move—because at the end of it all, you love God more than you fear man.

STILL FIGHTING YOUR OWN RECOVERY BATTLES?

If you're stuck in the middle of your own addiction, mental health problems, or suicidal thoughts, and you're still reading this book, my friend, I am celebrating your determination! Please do not give up. Never settle for anything less than the full measure of what the Father has for you—a promised-land life that's worth staying sober for and living to the fullest. Trust me, it's better than you could ever imagine!

This high-challenge call to Christian recovery leaders will be yours soon enough. A day is coming when you will know what it means to experience the loving embrace of the Father, empowering you to embrace others who are struggling and looking for redemption. I honor you, and I honor your journey. I can't wait to see what God will do in and through you!

RECOVERY BRINGS REVIVAL

I've said this several times already but it bears repeating: *Recovery is for everyone.* The sooner we, the church, understand this, the sooner our collective healing can begin.

We are all walking out our own journeys at different levels of awareness, but we all have identity issues that God will faithfully address if we give Him the opportunity. No matter how much identity work we've all done, we're all still in need of a Savior, Jesus. The hard heart work of the Uncovery isn't a tangible, step-by-step process that transforms the way the Christian church looks externally. It's an internal work that brings authentic, supernatural transformation one life at a time until we all experience the collective joy that's laid before us.

The promised-land life we're walking out together is, in essence, the kingdom of God. It's anywhere Jesus reigns supreme as Redeemer and King. It's a kingdom that's not of this world, but one we have access to here and now. All authority in heaven and on earth has been given to God's anointed Son. (See Matthew 28:18.) Jesus—our Master, Savior, Redeemer, and Friend—has secured a direct line to the Father on our behalf. We have access to the Father in the throne room of heaven, and we're seated with Jesus in heavenly places—right now.

> *Because of his great love for us, God, who is rich in mercy, made us alive with Christ even when we were dead in transgressions—it is by grace you have been saved. **And God raised us up with Christ and seated us with him in the heavenly realms in Christ Jesus,** in order that in the coming ages he might show the incomparable riches of his grace, expressed in his kindness to us in Christ Jesus. For it is by grace you have been saved, through faith—and this is not from yourselves, it is the gift of God—not by works, so that no one can boast. For we are God's handiwork, created in Christ Jesus to do good works, which God prepared in advance for us to do.*
>
> (Ephesians 2:4–10)

That same all-access pass to God isn't just available to us—it's available to the ones we're called to love and lead. To addicts. To the mentally ill. To the suicidal. To the lost. To the hurting. To the hopeless. To the confused. To leaders and followers, prisoners and captives, victims and abusers, sinners and saints. To every single one of the very least of these. Are you willing to invite them into the glory, the joy, and the hope you've tasted?

Be willing. I implore you, be willing. This journey through the wilderness and into a promised-land life worth staying sober for is an adventure you do not want to miss.

Recovery is the civil rights movement of our generation. And if we, the church, are willing to participate, I believe we will see revival rise up from the ashes of a reformed and refined recovery culture. It will be *real* revival—the kind where we are so filled to overflowing with God's love that it spills out of us effortlessly, drenching anyone who dares to lean in.

We'll see healing, deliverance, and transformation. We'll see families restored, lives rebuilt, and hearts fully reconciled to the Father. We'll see new leaders rise up, with less religious baggage, who will walk out the same authentic, simple faith that's been presented to them.

Embrace the Uncovery, and you'll see true revival come through the ones you love and lead. We who have been forgiven much love much—and as healed people, we will heal people when we do it in Jesus's name.

Lean in.

Get real.

Stay humble.

Go deeper.

Be strong and courageous.

Recover. Reform. Revive.

And soon you'll see, there's always more to uncover.

QUESTIONS FOR REFLECTION

1. In what ways might God be calling you to go deeper into *The Uncovery*? Are you willing? Why or why not?

_____

_____

_____

_____

_____

2. What are your biggest battles as you love and lead people in recovery or walk your own Uncovery journey? Are they the right battles?

_____

_____

_____

_____

_____

3. What does revival mean to you? Do you think recovery could be a catalyst toward it? Why or why not?

_____

_____

_____

_____

_____

ABOUT THE AUTHORS

GEORGE A. WOOD is an ordained minister, pastoral care counselor, recovery ministry founder, and recovery activist.

A former addict and suicide survivor, George has dedicated his life to radically grace-laced, Christ-centered recovery for people struggling with addiction, mental health problems, and suicidal thoughts.

He works tirelessly to bridge the gap between the spiritual and scientific communities to help people see recovery differently and build a new baseline for trauma-informed care.

A highly charismatic and sought-after teacher and preacher, George has become a nontraditional recovery authority through his radically divergent Timothy Initiative and Sober Truth Project ministries.

The Timothy Initiative is a faith-based ministry and open-ended program that works with men in addiction by providing safe housing and work opportunities. The Sober Truth Project aims to reshape how the world views addiction, mental health, people with suicidal thoughts, and the roles that faith, science, and trauma play in recovery to develop a more empathetic and loving society.

George studied business management at Binghamton and Morresville State universities in New York and mental health and Christian life coaching with the American Association of Christian Counselors. A certified addiction specialist, he is an ordained pastor and pastoral care counselor with Cornerstone Mission Family Church.

George lives in the inner city in Tampa, Florida, with his wife Julie and a community of brothers and sisters living out the gospel in a radical way. He has seen how the power of community can heal the trauma that causes addiction, mental health problems, and suicidal thoughts and is focused on mobilizing a generation of believers to go deeper into the Uncovery.

To connect with George, visit www.georgeawood.live.

BRIT EATON is a content strategist, writer, speaker, discipler, and all-around pursuer of the kingdom of God. She helps corporate, nonprofit, and ministry leaders find the words to say to move people to action.

An eager apostle and strong advocate for nontraditional recovery and women in ministry, Brit ministers in diverse, spirit-filled environments committed to unity in the body of Christ.

In addition to *The Uncovery: Understanding the Power of Community to Heal Trauma*, inspired by and developed with George Wood, she co-authored *Reckless Grace*, a book inspired by and developed with Bill Vanderbush.

Brit received a B.A. in Visual Communication from Mount Vernon Nazarene University, where she serves as an adjunct professor of business and marketing. She received her M.S. in marketing and communication, *summa cum laude*, from Franklin University. She also served in the U.S. Marine Corps Reserve.

Brit lives in a log home on ten wooded acres in Mount Vernon, Ohio, with her husband Mike and daughter Bella.

To connect with Brit, visit www.briteaton.com.

ABOUT THE TIMOTHY INITIATIVE

The Timothy Initiative (T.I.) is a radically divergent, Christ-centered recovery ministry that exists for broken, hurting men. It's an open-ended program that provides safe housing and work opportunities for these men while working through the Uncovery to discover what drove them to their struggles in the first place.

The sober-living community is designed to house and empower men in recovery for as long as it takes to help them build a promised-land life. In the face of addiction, homelessness, depression, mental health issues, suicidal thoughts, and incarceration, men are restored and healed through the power and love of Jesus Christ.

The ministry's four-pronged approach includes:

1. **Discipleship**. Those suffering from brokenness struggle to find healing and hope in light of their shortcomings and encounters with abuse in its various forms. T.I. men enter into an authentic, life-altering relationship with Jesus through prayer, Scripture studies, journaling, worship, mentorship, and service.

2. **Community.** Lasting recovery to overcome years of destructive behavior only happens within a community that provides accountability and encouragement. The men live together, eat together, and work together, celebrate victory and mourn loss together, and unite behind a common goal: to become devoted followers of Jesus.

3. **Recovery.** The Timothy Initiative's mission centers on seeing restoration in men seeking recovery by providing a comprehensive approach to addressing their every need—spiritual, physical, mental, and relational. They establish daily routines and learn new patterns of living to discover the love, freedom, identity, and fullness that only Jesus can bring.

4. **Work Therapy.** Work teaches trust and responsibility. As an extension of the T.I. community, it strengthens bonds and helps men break free from the bondage of selfishness. While working together and striving toward one common goal, they develop skills for future employment.

To learn more about the Timothy Initiative, visit www.timothyinitiative.org.

ABOUT THE SOBER TRUTH PROJECT

The Sober Truth Project is changing the way the world thinks about recovery, starting with the church. The ministry goes beyond traditional twelve-step programming to help struggling people not only *get sober* but also experience a total life transformation as they discover the truth about their identities as beloved children of a good Father God.

The ministry wants to end the message of shame that currently surrounds anyone in recovery, especially those affected by addiction, mental health struggles, or suicidal thoughts.

"Real recovery is the discovery of a person's God-given identity and learning what it means to walk in it for the rest of your life," says founder George A. Wood. Thus, recovery is for everyone.

The Sober Truth Project seeks to rebuild the message of recovery by engaging, educating, equipping, and empowering communities to develop a more empathetic and loving society that helps people realize a promised-land life.

To learn more about the Sober Truth Project, visit
www.sobertruthproject.org.

Welcome to Our House!

We Have a Special Gift for You

It is our privilege and pleasure to share in your love of Christian books. We are committed to bringing you authors and books that feed, challenge, and enrich your faith.

To show our appreciation, we invite you to sign up to receive a specially selected **Reader Appreciation Gift**, with our compliments. Just go to the Web address at the bottom of this page.

God bless you as you seek a deeper walk with Him!

WE HAVE A GIFT FOR YOU. VISIT:

whpub.me/nonfictionthx

WHITAKER
HOUSE